Praise for 'Dying to Live'

"If you ever doubted how serious a disease Covid-19 is, please read this book. Grant and Amanda have written a powerful account of his journey from working as a clinician preparing for the pandemic, to becoming ill, spending almost two months on life support, and then the long road to recovery. This is a personal story but it is also a rallying call for continued and expanded investment in the NHS, public health and disease prevention."

Professor Linda Bauld, Bruce and John Usher Chair in Public Health, University of Edinburgh

"This is a true story of courage, dedication and skill. Professor Grant McIntyre, writing clearly and from his own experience, recounts what it is like to suffer the ravaging effects of Covid-19 and to recover. His praise for the compassion and skill of the NHS staff who cared for him is truly well deserved. Read this book. You will be better for having done so."

Terry Waite CBE

"Grant and Amanda's words pick you up from your normal life and transport you into their world. It is a story of hope, of worry, of loss and of gain. A story that needs to be told and read."

Dr Matt Morgan, intensive care consultant, researcher and author of *Critical* (2019)

"This story is a testament to individual strength and determination, not only of Grant, Amanda and the wider family, but also that of the numerous healthcare professionals who give their all every day. As Grant alludes to, the NHS will always be there 'Per Ardua' – through adversity, and beyond."

Dr Pauline Austin and Dr Stephen Cole, consultants in anaesthesia and intensive care medicine

At the start of 2020, Grant McIntyre was a fit and healthy 49-year-old. The year had started unusually, with reports of a new virus sweeping across the world. At the end of March, life changed suddenly for the McIntyre family as Grant tested positive for COVID-19 and was admitted to hospital. As the days passed, the situation became progressively worse. Grant's body went into a cytokine storm and this immune response nearly killed him. He suffered multi-organ failure, a collapsed lung and sepsis, spending fifty days on ECMO life support which no one, not even the doctors, expected him to survive. As his condition deteriorated, death looked almost certain. This is the *inspiring* story of his journey back to life.

'DYING TO LIVE'

The Story of Grant McIntyre,

Covid's Sickest Patient

GRANT MCINTYRE

&

AMANDA MCINTYRE

TIPPERMUIR
· BOOKS LIMITED ·

'Dying to Live': The Story of Grant McIntyre, Covid's Sickest Patient.
Copyright © Grant & Amanda McIntyre 2021. All rights reserved.

This first edition published and copyright 2021 by
Tippermuir Books Ltd, Perth, Scotland.
mail@tippermuirbooks.co.uk – www.tippermuirbooks.co.uk.

ISBN 978-1-913836-09-2 (paperback).

ISBN 978-1-913836-11-5 (eBook).

A CIP catalogue record for this book is available from the British Library.
Editorial and Project coordination by Dr Paul S Philippou.
Cover design by Matthew Mackie.
Editorial support: Jean Hands and Steve Zajda.

Thanks go to NHS Tayside, STV News, DC Thomson, the BBC and
Amanda McIntyre for permission to use the photographs in the book.

Text layout and artwork by Bernard Chandler [graffik].
Text set in Melior LT Std 10.2/14pt with Melior Bold titling.

Printed and bound by Ashford Colour Press Ltd, Gosport, Hampshire, PO13 0FW

Dedication

This book is dedicated to the people around the world who have suffered from the effects of COVID, to those who mourn the loss of someone who didn't survive and to those who continue to work tirelessly to save and rebuild lives affected by this wretched disease.

Acknowledgements

It goes without saying that we are indebted to our family and friends for supporting us throughout one of the most difficult periods of our life together. Around the globe, family, friends and strangers came together in words, thoughts, prayers and deeds to keep us going at every stage in the journey. We truly appreciate every single visit and phone call as well as all the food, cards, flowers, gifts, emails, messages and social media comments when my life was held in the balance. We acknowledge everyone who took care of us during my illness and as I recovered. Our work colleagues in education, dentistry and orthodontics, both locally and globally, have been a tower of strength and the kindness shown by my present and former patients has been truly humbling. We simply could not have made the journey without you and we thank you all from the bottom of our hearts.

This book is the culmination of that difficult journey and would not have been possible without the support of so many people. To the rehabilitation team in hospital who suggested we write a book on our experiences to those who helped with the information, detail and encouragement, we thank you all. It has been a cathartic experience to relive some difficult memories and to discover some of those that we were protected from. We are grateful to our brother-in-law, Douglas, our publisher Paul Philippou and one of the most gifted and compassionate consultants ever, Pauline Austin, for being our 'critical friends' while writing and revising the text. Our publisher, Tippermuir Books and Paul Philippou in particular have been encouraging and honest whilst helping us work towards the final text, looking after us at every stage in the publishing journey from draft to book. We hope you, the reader, find something of interest in our story and thank you for taking the time to read it.

List of Chapters

Foreword

IT WAS IN the middle of December 2019 when as a group of Intensive Care Unit (ICU) consultants in the north east of Scotland, we first became aware of stories of a new type of pneumonia in China. At the time, it seemed so remote and far away. I don't think any of us had the faintest idea of what was to come. The last 18 months has turned all of our lives upside down. For each and every one of us there have undoubtedly been many moments where the surreal reality of living during a global pandemic and in lockdown has felt like something out of a disaster movie.

As we moved into the first few weeks of 2020, the ever-increasing barrage of reports detailing the infective nature and severity of this novel illness was a wake-up call to us, and to the rest of the world. It rapidly became clear that this wasn't SARS or MERS, of which we had all been aware but thankfully not directly exposed to; neither was it Ebola. It was the same virus that can cause the common cold, yet somehow it was causing complete chaos.

In Dundee, with our nearest infectious disease intensive care unit in Edinburgh, we hoped it would not darken our door. Our naïve expectation was that as Covid patients were admitted in Dundee, they would simply be transferred to Edinburgh, but our thoughts were sadly way off the mark.

If there is one thing the doctors, nurses and indeed all dedicated NHS staff can do, it is rise to a challenge. We saw and heard the calls from Italy to make preparations, and so we did. We had time to plan, and plan we did – endlessly and repetitively. We developed a plan on a Monday, edited it Tuesday and Wednesday, ripped it up on Thursday and started again on Friday, Saturday and Sunday.

The Scottish Government worked closely with the ICU community, trying to source large numbers of ventilators, monitors and dialysis machines. The problem was that the rest of the world also wanted this equipment and without delay. Long lists of extra equipment were drawn up and items were sourced from across the hospital and beyond. We repurposed anaesthetic machines to ventilate patients but quickly realised there were huge flaws with that plan as well.

We were asked to double, treble and then ultimately quadruple intensive care ventilated bed capacity as the political mantra was that 'no one would die from Covid-19 due to the lack of an ICU bed'. This was not an easy feat and necessitated the commandeering of operating theatre and recovery space to cope with the anticipated demand.

What the politicians really didn't understand was who would look after these patients. The well-established and very necessary high ratio of nursing staff to critically ill patients was to be diluted with less experienced staff redeployed to the Covid-19 'frontline'. It was unknown what competencies these individuals had, and how we, or more importantly our ICU nursing colleagues, would cope with this significant change as well as with the added burden of treating a disease we had never seen before.

Chinese and Italian officials led us to believe it was a respiratory system disease but it clearly wasn't. It soon became apparent that it wasn't 'just a cold' as one of our colleagues had remarked early in the year. This was a disease that would wreak havoc across every system of the body and bring us to question the very foundations of our intensive care practice.

The first wave was met with a real 'call to arms'. The atmosphere in the hospital in those early days of preparation was almost one of excitement. The camaraderie and enthusiasm was immense and great things were quickly achieved to allow us to safely treat those who came through the doors both with and without Covid-19. This teamwork and mutual respect amongst healthcare professionals succeeded in making the dark days that little bit less gloomy. Things just happened, without the usual Byzantine process of committees and people working in silos blind to the priorities of those working outside of their immediate area.

We could, however, only do this by pausing almost the entire activity of the rest of the hospital. Elective surgery stopped, outpatient clinics were postponed or moved to a virtual platform and even some cancer work was deferred. We became by default the 'Covid NHS' with all the immense power and expertise of the NHS dedicated and focused onto fighting one single disease.

There were gloomy days, and many of them. As a critical care community our whole way of working had changed and the relationships we build with families on a daily basis were no longer easy to forge. Getting to know our patients and hear about them from the person at the bedside had disappeared overnight. It was replaced with a poor substitute – video calls. We will never again underestimate the value of face-to-face contact with family members and the importance of them seeing first-hand their loved one, and the lengths to which ICU teams strive to keep them alive.

Whilst the number and intensity of patients may have differed across the UK, what didn't differ was the impressive and timely response to getting us out of the situation. Clinical research grew at an astounding rate, rapidly giving us answers to the myriad of questions we had. Science ensured the vaccination programme would keep pace and the benefits of this are now being realised.

Now, in 2021 as vaccination rates increase and we head out of the second/third waves into the summer, the UK feels like a different place. It is fair to say that at the start of last autumn and winter we knew there would be a resurgence but none of us really thought it would surpass the first wave. That time though, we had a head start. We had more tools in our armamentarium and although by then we were all very weary, we pulled together to get through the winter and can today see a brighter future ahead.

As we write this, it is sadly clear that not everywhere is experiencing the same improving trajectory. Cases are exploding in India and oxygen supplies are woefully inadequate or even non-existent for the many hundreds of critically ill patients. Once again there are more lives being lost and the journey to beat Covid-19 into remission continues.

This book is one man's personal account of his journey. A man who is a healthcare professional, a scientist and a colleague. It is his direct and personal experience of Covid-19 and is a timely reminder to us all of the fragility of life.

This story is a testament to individual strength and determination, not only of Grant, Amanda and the wider family, but also that of the numerous healthcare professionals who give their all every day. As Grant alludes to, the NHS will always be there 'Per Ardua' – through adversity, and beyond.

Dr Pauline Austin and Dr Stephen Cole,
Consultants in Anaesthesia and Intensive Care Medicine,
Ninewells Hospital, Dundee

May 2021

———————————

Introduction

AT THE START of 2020, I was a fit and healthy 49-year-old consultant and Professor of Orthodontics at Dundee Dental Research Hospital & School. My wife Amanda, a primary school head teacher, and I had been married for six months and were quietly getting on with our lives and respective careers. Our four adult children were slowly moving on in life and becoming independent. 2020 was to be a quiet year for us and along with our young Labrador, Sherlock Bones, we planned trips to France to search for our perfect holiday home and dreamed of holidays in the sun sipping vin rouge and nibbling Brie, Mont d'Or, Camembert and other delicious cheeses.

The year had started unusually for everyone worldwide with news reports being filled with concern about a new virus that had caused chaos in a Chinese city, which then swept across the rest of the world and subsequently paralysed many countries. Our professional lives became even busier with constant reference to risk assessments and herd immunity; and new words started to permeate our vocabulary with terms such as 'self-isolate' and 'PPE' becoming part of everyday conversation.

At the end of March, life changed suddenly for the family as I tested positive for COVID-19 and was admitted to hospital for the third time in a week with my life held in the balance. Life for us changed irrevocably and it was suddenly all about survival. Nobody knew what was to come and even the doctors, who we all turn to in our time of medical need, did not have any answers. As the days went on, the news became darker and darker. My body's cytokine storm immune response nearly killed me outright. I suffered a number of medical complications including multi-organ failure, a collapsed lung and sepsis while in intensive care.

I spent 50 days on Extracorporeal Membrane Oxygenation (ECMO) life support which no one, not even the doctors fighting to keep me alive, expected me to survive, or have a normal quality of life even if I did. As my condition deteriorated, death was looking almost certain and Amanda had to prepare for the worst.

This is the story of that horrific journey, multiple near-death experiences and our perspectives on surviving critical illness along with the UK and global story. To date, I remain the sickest survivor of COVID-19 in Scotland and one of a small group of patients in the UK who were lucky to recover from death's door after being on life support. I am proud of the rehabilitation I have made and the strength of my family to overcome such a difficult time in our lives. My life was not only saved but rebuilt by my NHS heroes and whilst I still have some problems with my respiratory health, I don't plan to let these get in the way of enjoying the rest of my life. The support I received from my tremendous family, particularly Amanda, along with friends and colleagues across the globe enabled me to make this miraculous recovery and I owe it to everyone involved to make sure I live!

This book will open your eyes to the personal story of a family who, despite all the odds, were victorious in the conquest of a vicious infective disease with the help of our incredible NHS. I am humbled to have been looked after by such an incredible team, none of whom thought I would still be here. I hope you find this, our story, to be of interest alongside your own journey through the difficult time the COVID-19 pandemic has caused.

Grant McIntyre, April 2021

CHAPTER 1

I am Going to Die

'I AM GOING TO DIE, PLEASE SAVE MY LIFE' were the words I said to the Intensive Care Unit (ICU) consultant on what was to become the most difficult period of my life. I had no idea at that point the havoc that COVID-19 was going to wreak on my body and my life.

In March 2020, I had been going to work as normal but I was starting to feel strange. I lost my appetite and began to feel increasingly unwell over a period of several days. I gradually became colder and colder and started to feel that I was becoming sick. My feet were as cold as ice. I couldn't seem to focus and as the days drew on, the fatigue increased. This was unusual as I am not typically troubled by the cold and can only remember having the flu once in my life.

People joke that you only have the real flu when you are self-employed or if you cannot pick up a tenner lying on the floor beside the bed. When I had the flu many years ago it was the Christmas holidays. I was not very sociable and spent many heavy days in bed. My arms were like lead and my feet felt like concrete. I recall having to carefully plan each trip to the bathroom as my head and joints ached so badly. Minimising the number of steps seemed key. I knew on this occasion that I did not have the flu, I simply felt rubbish. Several of my work colleagues were feeling run-down as well. It seemed likely that we had all picked up the same bug but what was it?

Having no appetite was very out of character. I knew something was not right as I normally clear my plate just like our Labrador, Sherlock Bones. At work, I felt dreadful while trying to lead the management team through a difficult period. Many of the staff were now off sick and we did not know who was going to come in each day. Others were wondering if they should report for duty or stay at home. We therefore started standing huddle meetings round a whiteboard to determine who would be at work each day. On the third day of feeling poorly, I knew I couldn't stand and slid to the floor at the morning meeting. I noted that several of my managerial colleagues were not well either. It was a strange time at work as nothing was normal. The usual human resources policies were not particularly useful and I was being asked to provide answers to questions that had not been asked before. I spent most of that day in my office trying to solve problems for everyone else whilst trying to ignore my own body which was aching. The heater in the corner of my office was on at the full setting and while it was heating the air, it wasn't warming me up. I simply didn't recognise that I had a raging temperature. Various people came to my office during the day and commented that it was roasting hot. I couldn't feel any heat and was chilled to the bone.

As a bi-phasic sleeper, I sometimes have a little daytime nap at work to revive me. On that ill-fated day, I had a longer than average sleep on my office floor. I woke up feeling rough and after a short period of time I decided to call it a day and went home. Anything on my desk could wait until the next day and I would deal with it then. My desk was untidy with papers and the laptop was left as it was, plugged in. I was too fatigued to pick it up and take it home. This was one evening where I would not be working at home. I walked slowly to my car and felt exhausted. It took me a few minutes to recover the energy to start driving. How I drove home without incident baffled me. I had to concentrate so hard to focus on driving a journey I had made a thousand times. I had originally arranged to meet friends for a beer at our local craft

'DYING TO LIVE'

brewery pub. It is a friendly little place and very 'artisanal' with seats made from pallets and couches no doubt from charity shops. The kegs are not hidden as in other pubs but are fixed onto the back wall with a slate denoting the contents. I am not a regular at the pub by any means so an evening with the lads is a treat. I was not the designated driver yet I could not face alcohol that evening. I had no choice but to call off since I was by now feeling dreadful. My friends were therefore duly concerned for my welfare and sent me all sorts of text messages chastising me and winding me up. At the time I thought, I don't mind - I will have plenty of opportunities to return the favour. Although it was spring, I insisted on having the log fire on at home as I was frozen. I lay on the sofa for a while. The television was a blur. I couldn't process any information. I had never felt like this before, so I went to bed early, fully clothed and complaining of the cold. Amanda, kept insisting that I had a temperature. I couldn't see it. I was so cold!

It was a rough night's sleep and I got up late the next morning. I had tossed and turned all night and I felt like a deflated beach ball. My breathing was not normal and I couldn't catch my breath. I knew that I could not go to work for the first time in my career. I asked Amanda to call in sick for me. I could not make the call as I was too unwell. Guilt racked me, having not missed a day of work since graduating from university 27 years earlier. More importantly, we had been investing considerable amounts of time at work preparing for the expected COVID-19 pandemic. I had had a major involvement in the plans for transforming the physical and human resources so that any risk of transmission between patients or staff would be minimised, whilst continuing to provide patients with good care. Who would run our building and who would take care of the arrangements that had to be made that day?

I was not able to inflate my lungs properly, which was new, and I still felt frozen and was now light-headed. What was going on? Did I have the flu? I wondered when this would pass and when I would return to normal. Not soon enough I said to myself. I felt floored. I needed help from Amanda to get dressed during the morning and get down the stairs. Even with additional layers of clothing, I was horribly cold as I sat on the sofa hunched forwards to try to get as much air into my lungs as possible. I felt truly dreadful and was now concerned that I had contracted COVID-19, the virus that was rampaging through Europe having been first detected in Wuhan, China. Furthermore, I was becoming increasingly concerned about my breathlessness. It was a worrying feeling, and it crept over me insidiously. While I thought I was having an asthma attack by late morning, my various asthma inhalers were not at all helpful. Although I have had mild asthma since my late teenage years, I had never been truly unwell with asthma nor had an asthma attack. I knew I was needing help. Why couldn't I breathe properly? Nothing was working and I was deteriorating as the clock ticked and the hours passed. By now, I had spent several hours on the sofa, struggling for breath and was not comfortable either sitting up and hunched forwards, or lying down. My breathing was bad in any position. I could not get any air into my airways.

I was 49 and relatively fit and healthy. Usually I deal with colds or sneezes with a concoction of an antihistamine tablet and ibuprofen and a large glass of whisky to help me into a long, deep, restorative sleep. The whisky has to be Scotch of course, not that other genres are inferior, but as a Scot, I only drink the fermented and distilled variety that is produced in my own country. My preference is Macallan, an excellent Speyside malt that is best imbibed neat for maximum enjoyment. A whisky or even a hot toddy was out of the question. I realised that I needed more help than that.

By early afternoon, Amanda and her daughter Anna, were becoming increasingly concerned about me and I reluctantly allowed them to call the emergency service, NHS 24. I do not like unnecessary attention when other people are likely to need help and was annoyed at myself for being unwell. I knew I was not able to be a useful husband or father and had left my work colleagues in the lurch at a crucial time. Who was going to deal with what was on my desk today? It took nearly an hour for the phone call to be answered as the service was swamped with calls, many of them about COVID-19. The call handler advised Amanda to keep me upright and take additional doses of my asthma medication, particularly the salbutamol reliever inhaler. I went along with this but it didn't help and Amanda asked for an ambulance to come to the house.

Amanda phoned my brother John, a GP, who was very supportive but as he was at work, there was no immediate solution he could offer. My sister-in-law, his wife, who is a nurse and treats asthma patients, suggested Amanda try to help my breathing by keeping me sitting upright and that she buy a small pulse-oximeter device to measure my heart rate and blood oxygen levels in case I deteriorated as time went on. Amanda duly ordered this online. I was still sitting up with my arms stretching my lungs to try to breathe but there was nothing else we could do except wait for help to arrive.

About 45 minutes later, a lovely ambulance crew arrived and before they could come into the house, they needed to find out what was happening. Amanda mentioned to them that I might have COVID-19 and as they had not encountered a potential COVID-19 patient before, this was their first experience of donning their full personal protective equipment (PPE). It seemed to take forever for the paramedics to enter the house but then two astronauts arrived in the living room startling me. I knew they weren't from NASA but I still found it difficult to communicate with them.

'Ground Control to Major Tom' is a joke that regularly trips off my tongue when my kids don't listen to me, but this was no time for jokes. I couldn't even think straight far less joke. By this point, I was sitting forwards, hunched further to try to get as much oxygen in my lungs as possible. I was wearing a hat, scarf, thick jumper and I had a blanket over me despite the fact that our enormous log burner was at full blast. I was struggling for oxygen and it was apparent to everyone.

The ambulance crew assessed my major organs, checked my heart with an ECG tracing, and excluded a cardiac event such as a heart attack immediately, thankfully. They assessed my lungs and noted that I was by no means breathing normally. At the same time, they checked my blood glucose level in case I was diabetic or suffering from critical illness and took my pulse, oxygen saturation level and blood pressure. Although my blood glucose level was normal, my other blood signs were not, particularly my blood oxygen saturation level which had dropped to 88%. It should be 95% or greater. I knew this was not good news but had no idea of its significance. The crew administered oxygen immediately.

The ambulance crew did not want to leave me at home and insisted I went to hospital. They couldn't do anything to help me, which was perplexing. I hoped that there would be treatments to help me breathe more easily at the hospital. They helped me walk into the ambulance and going outside the house felt like going into a freezer. As I sat in the ambulance, I still felt the cold chill my entire body, even with a blanket. John, one of the ambulance technicians, sat with me in the back of the ambulance and tried to comfort me. It was a strange journey and I felt horrible. John gave me sips of water to drink but I could hardly hold the cup. I couldn't see much out of the windows because of where I was sitting but I knew the roads well, travelling the same route to work every day.

I could recognise the tops of buildings and landmarks and the journey seemed fairly swift. I remember saying to John that I hoped I wasn't wasting anyone's time. He replied that I was unwell and needed medical help. He was kind even though I knew this scenario was new to him and must have been worrying for both of the crew.

The ambulance crew took me to the main city hospital, which is one of the hospitals I had worked in for over 20 years. I had been involved in the plans in the weeks before to split the hospital into COVID-19 and non-COVID-19 sides, with little potential for patients and staff to cross-contaminate. I was not regularly in the areas designated as COVID-19 'hot' areas but knew the layout of the hospital well and recognised some of the staff. Increasingly, I realised that this might not be a 24-hour cold or the flu and I would need medical assistance to fight this. I was admitted to the COVID-19 assessment ward, which was used normally as an infectious diseases ward, and was given a side-room overlooking the ambulance bay. The side-room was a negative pressure room so each time the door opened there was a rush of air, which was weird, and it felt like death itself was breathing on me.

Although I worked in the hospital, I hadn't had an overnight hospital stay since I was a child and it all seemed surreal. I was given a packet of cheese sandwiches and a cup of tea. Hardly a substantial meal, but I didn't want anything to eat so I ate part of one of the sandwiches with difficulty. The doctor came to see me during the evening and explained that he would run a series of tests including a COVID-19 swab of my nose and throat. He was a lovely Australian chap who had relocated to the UK. We had a brief conversation about the potential implications of Brexit on Australians working in the UK. The blood tests were straightforward, and the repeat blood pressure and pulse were normal. More importantly, my blood oxygen levels had improved to 95%. I was pleased that my blood oxygen level had improved from earlier in the day. The COVID-19 nasal swab was extremely unpleasant, and I felt the end of the swab going far up my nose and wondered if it would end up in my brain. The throat swab was okay by comparison. I let Amanda know that I was settled for the evening and turned the light out. I could not, however, turn off the noise of the busy ward outside. Furthermore, the room was directly above the COVID-19 'front door' and all night I heard ambulances delivering multiple suspected COVID-19 cases to the hospital. I wondered if they were more ill than me. It was a strange night and all night I contemplated the condition of each new patient as each ambulance drew up.

Although there was little chance of a good sleep, I did the best I could and cat-napped all night. I was awoken in the morning with the nursing staff going about their daily routine. My breathing was by no means normal but felt better than the previous day. I had a simple breakfast of porridge and tea. I took a shower. Luckily, there was a chair in the shower as I felt unsteady on my feet. Getting dressed was a struggle. Several of my colleagues had messaged me to find out if I was okay. As I felt better than the day before, I let them know I would need a few days off and would return to work the next week. Another good friend of over 20 years, Piers, also sent me various messages of 'concern', knowing that I was unwell. He and I regularly exchange various cheeky messages, winding each other up mercilessly. At one point, he asked me if my coffin had been measured up. Naturally, I responded to confirm that Piers wouldn't have been invited to the funeral if I was dead.

The consultant in charge of the ward came to see me. She sat down on the edge of the bed and explained that whilst the COVID-19 test result would take several hours to come, it was highly likely that I was positive. She explained to me that if the test was positive, I would need to isolate and keep away from the rest of the family to avoid them catching the virus from me. I was to be discharged with steroids to help my breathing and antibiotics to deal with any bacterial infection. I was to rest at home until better. I waited for the prescription drugs to be issued by the nurses. Amanda came to pick me up and I was walked out to the car wearing a mask and feeling unsteady on my feet. I remember the journey back home being rather strange as I could not focus on the farms and buildings we passed. I went straight to the lounge when we reached home and was not interested in lunch. I tried to watch the log fire but was too tired to focus properly.

Mid-afternoon, my mobile phone sitting on the sofa beside me rang and I answered it immediately. I knew it would be the result of the COVID-19 test. The infectious diseases doctor explained that my swabs were positive and that my family and I should self-isolate for two weeks and not leave the house unless in an exceptional circumstance. Fortunately, Amanda had been shopping the day before I went into hospital, so there would be enough food for the two of us and my adult stepchildren, Jonathan and Anna, and my son, Colin, who lives between our house and his mother's house. Our fourth child, Alexander, now lived in his own flat. A close work friend, Kunal, a cancer surgeon, texted to see how I was, and offered to deliver anything we needed as a family, including toilet roll. I was puzzled about this and didn't know that over the few days since becoming unwell that toilet roll had become in short supply as people stockpiled. I did not feel like any food later in the day and went to bed early. I was still cold and struggling to breathe.

I do not remember anything of the next day except still being incredibly breathless. Even going to the bathroom took what seemed an inordinate amount of planning and energy. I wasn't able to think straight and both Amanda and Anna continued to be worried. I lay in bed all day and drifted in and out of sleep and semi-consciousness. I ate nothing all day. Unfortunately, the steroids and salbutamol asthma inhaler did little to help. My brother and sister-in-law were naturally concerned. By the evening, my breathing was again severely laboured, and I was sitting up in bed periodically with my shoulders forward to try to gasp some air. Amanda and Anna became increasingly worried about me. They called NHS 24 again and a second ambulance was requested. The ambulance paramedics were told by Amanda that I was positive for COVID-19 and they came into the house wearing full PPE. The astronauts ran the same series of tests as the previous ambulance crew and I was taken back to the hospital that I knew so well.

This time I was taken to the same ward as previously but rather than being put in a side-room, I was put in a bay with five other patients. I knew that it was the middle of the night when I was admitted and I didn't like the notion of disturbing the other patients from sleeping. I was given oxygen to help me breathe and observations were recorded by the nurses every hour. After a poor night's sleep, the ward consultant came to see me in the morning. My observations had improved overnight which was a relief. I was again discharged with steroids and advised to use the salbutamol inhaler to help my breathing as needed. Amanda came and collected me again and I felt a sense of *déjà vu* as I was pushed out to the car in a wheelchair wearing a mask and we travelled back home again. I went straight to bed when we arrived home and again the fatigue meant that I was unable to be of any help around the house and was again either sleeping or on the borderline of being unconscious. I don't remember much of the day or evening.

Over the next 48 hours I did not leave the bedroom except to use the bathroom. I have no memory of eating anything. By day six since initially feeling unwell, I was relatively oblivious as to what was going on around me. Amanda and Anna called NHS 24 again and based on my condition, an advanced paramedic was dispatched to come to see me. It was the middle of the night. He arrived promptly and was concerned about my condition and within a few minutes, he was making phone calls. The issue was whether to admit me to an infectious diseases ward or through A&E. He summoned the third ambulance to arrive at our house in a week.

The ambulance came swiftly and the crew came into the bedroom dressed once more in the now ubiquitous astronaut outfits. There was no fuss and they wanted to take me to hospital as quickly as possible. I remember being placed into the wheelchair and being bumped down the stairs before being lifted into the ambulance and lying down on the stretcher. The cold air froze me instantly and all I could think about was feeling frozen and concentrating on each and every breath.

I don't remember much of the journey back to the hospital. I needed a fair amount of oxygen to help me breathe. I could see the reflection of the blue ambulance lights from windows as we passed buildings. It felt like a swift journey. I was no longer a consultant. I was now a patient and a very sick patient at that. In the end I was admitted directly to the ward. The oxygen therapy continued overnight with a nasal cannula. I now had a significant fever. The consultant came to see me during the night and it was comforting that he was also a professor with whom I had done research work in the past. He ran a series of tests and this time a chest X-ray was taken. I was not fit enough to go to the X-ray department so a mobile X-ray machine came to me. An imaging plate was placed against my back and, as I was weak, two nurses helped me sit up in the bed for this. I thought it rather ironic that the radiographer shouted 'stand clear, X-rays' when taking the image as all the other patients were asleep!

The consultant waited to see the X-ray image and I knew that this meant he was expecting bad news. He told me that it showed severe viral pneumonia. This was not good news. Amanda had suffered pneumonia on two occasions in recent years. She knew she was unwell on both occasions but it took a chest X-ray to diagnose her pneumonia each time. Luckily it cleared up with antibiotics on both occasions and I hoped this episode of pneumonia would resolve quickly for me too. He left the bedside and I drifted off into semi-consciousness again. Later on in the night, a junior doctor came and inserted a line in one of the veins in my right arm and a nurse administered antibiotics. The ward was noisy but this was not the cause of the strange night to come.

During the night, I had various delusional thoughts about dying. I was used to discussing the possibility of death with patients when they were being prepared for surgery but I had not expected to confront the death question myself for many years yet. I wondered what was happening to me. I was confused and could feel my heart racing. At one point, I had an out-of-body experience. I floated above the bed looking down on a lifeless body below. I wondered if I had now died. I drifted vertically and as I went higher, I became more distant from the life that I had known and I could not snap out of the scariest nightmare in my whole life. Looking back, I wonder if I was closer to several relatives who had passed away, including my father who had tragically died of a heart attack when I was 19. I had started to wonder if I would soon be reunited with him. Although I am a Christian, I did not feel that this was the time to ask God for forgiveness and to be given the chance to live. Perhaps I would have if I had been able to think straight. It might have been a good idea had I known what was to come.

I somehow gave myself a shake immediately afterwards and felt extremely traumatised by what was happening to me. I now knew that I was seriously ill and decided to sit the hospital bed up and focus on breathing just as my sister-in-law had advised several days earlier. I suspected if I went to sleep I might not wake up. It took me back to being a child where I used to lie awake on many nights wondering how as humans we 'remember' to breathe while asleep. Although I learned how the body worked at university, I didn't want to put any trust in my failing body, which I felt was playing tricks on me. I was alone and knew that I could not think properly. It was clear to me that I had to concentrate on breathing slowly and continually. It was the worst night of my life and I was terrified about my worsening condition. Kunal texted me around 5am to ask how I was; he starts work early. Somehow, I replied to let him know that I was sick but I would soon be home after treatment. I managed to stay conscious by concentrating on my breathing even though this was worsening by the hour. I wondered if there was anything that would help my now dreadful condition. Having briefly thought back to the documents I had seen at work in the previous week looking for staff to be redeployed to COVID-19 pressure points in the hospital, I now realised that I was a deteriorating patient and the deterioration was not only progressive, but fast.

I was confused because I could not breathe properly and I was aware of the concern among the nursing staff over my oxygen levels. My observations had been recorded every hour overnight and I had acknowledged this was not customary and they were doing this because I was in a bad way. The nursing and medical staff did not share the results with me but I knew they were concerned about what they were finding each hour. The morning couldn't come quickly enough. I passed on breakfast but kept using the salbutamol inhaler to try to help me breathe. It was futile. Fortunately, the morning ward round was early and I was relieved to see the doctors at the end of the bay. I could see that they were discussing the patients before coming to each bedside. They seemed to be discussing me for much longer than anyone else before coming to my bed. There wasn't much discussion with me as I couldn't breathe to speak to the team clearly. I knew my condition would worsen further without a change in the treatment and I struggled to explain that I could feel a rapid decline and that I would die without extensive medical intervention. It was a calm conversation and I was surprised that I was not distressed at all. Surely people become agitated when death is imminent? I wondered if I was not dying after all but was simply confused. The hospital had allocated a specific high dependency unit (HDU) and intensive care unit for COVID-19 patients to be on ventilators and I had also read on the Internet over the previous week about the benefits of continuous positive airway pressure (CPAP) to help lungs recover when affected by COVID-19 pneumonia. I knew Mercedes and Ferrari had switched car production to ventilator manufacture so hopefully there would be enough available in hospitals around the world by now.

I asked the consultant to put me on a CPAP machine as I was worried about the seriousness of my condition. After what seemed a short conversation I was swiftly being transferred to HDU. A charming consultant, Dr McLow, came to see me and I said to him, 'I think I am going to die, please save my life'. These words will stay with me for the rest of my life and I am glad that I was so candid. I wanted to be put on CPAP, and fast.

It hit me how serious my condition now was. Death was imminent without life-saving treatment. There was no time to lose. Dr McLow was reassuring and mentioned that he would get everything ready for me. Within a few minutes, he and a colleague in full PPE reappeared, a needle and cannula were inserted into a vein in my left arm. I was ready to be anaesthetised. I was scared about what was yet to come and although I felt the anaesthetic drug gently flow up the veins in my left arm, I was unconscious within seconds.

To this day, I am haunted by guilt that there was no time to tell my family how much I loved them. I said to myself, 'You can fight this'. How I would mount a fight to this infection was beyond me at that point and my final thought was that it would be the fight of my life, but little did I know that this was to become my fight for life.

———————————

CHAPTER 2

Why all the Fuss about Covid-19?

THE TECHNICAL NAME for COVID-19 is SARS-CoV-2 virus, severe acute respiratory syndrome coronavirus 2. Its story began with a cluster of dozens of cases of pneumonia of unknown origin in Wuhan, Hubei Province, China, which was reported by the Chinese Center for Disease Control and Prevention at the end of 2019. This was formally alerted to the World Health Authority (WHO) soon afterwards. News agencies around the globe started to cover the story instantly and there was an opinion that the relatively closed structure of Chinese society and the government-controlled and censored Chinese media were suppressing information that would be of value to humanity and the rest of the world. At the start of January 2020, censorship of vital health information relating to this emerging crisis, which should have been freely shared worldwide was confirmed when the Central Hospital of Wuhan banned all staff from commenting publicly on the disease or making any recordings or images of Covid patients.

After lobbying, the Chinese government agreed to accept a WHO scientific team to aid the work being carried out by their own research team and in early January, Chinese state media reported the death of the first patient from the illness caused by the virus. He was a 61-year-old man who had been a regular visitor to the market in Wuhan and had been diagnosed with abdominal tumours and chronic liver disease. Neither age nor his medical condition were in his favour. A novel coronavirus was formally identified within samples obtained from cases and the initial assessment of the viral genetic sequences indicated that this had caused the outbreak. The Coronavirus Study Group of the International Committee on Taxonomy of Viruses named the agent SARS-CoV-2 in their paper 'Severe acute respiratory syndrome-related coronavirus: The species and its viruses – a statement of the Coronavirus Study Group' and full characterisation of the virus continues today.

I was interested in what was going on at an early stage as I work with a mathematician, Pang Lang, who is originally from Wuhan and has a number of family members who still live there. Pang was naturally concerned for his family and friends and I did my best to let him know that they were in my thoughts, although there was little else I could do. He would normally go back to Wuhan a few times each year, however his latest trip was clearly off limits. My brother Callum also spent Christmas 2019 in Hong Kong and little was open due to the outbreak having reached there so he spent most of his time trapped in his hotel room.

The suspicions that the Chinese authorities were trying to suppress the news about this new disease were further confirmed when reporters from Hong Kong who were trying to film the situation within Wuhan Central Hospital were taken to the local police station for questioning. The first confirmed cases outside mainland China (in Japan, South Korea and Thailand) were made public by the WHO in late January, and the first case of the virus in the West popped up in Washington State where a man in his thirties developed symptoms, having just returned from a trip to Wuhan.

Surprisingly, Public Health England announced at this point that it was only moving the risk level for the UK from 'very low' to 'low'. Little did they know at that point what was yet to unfold, or what was to happen to their agency. Furthermore, it is unfortunate that it took the Chinese authorities several weeks to accept WHO help and it is likely that this allowed the initial cases to spread uncontrolled within the Wuhan population and beyond. The new virus causing the wide spectrum of disease was formally named by the WHO in February as COVID-19 (an acronym formed from 'CO' for corona, 'VI' for virus, 'D' for disease and 19 for '2019').

Drastic action had by then been taken by the Chinese authorities. The 11 million population of Wuhan was cut off from the rest of China. All flights and trains into and out of Wuhan were cancelled and bus transport along with ferries and the subway within the city of Wuhan were suspended. By this point 17 people had died and there were 570 known infected cases across Taiwan, Japan, Thailand, South Korea and the US. Figures released by the Chinese National Railway Administration indicated that approximately 100,000 people had left by train before the deadline. Construction began on a specialist emergency hospital in Wuhan at the beginning of February 2020. News media across the globe carried reports of the hospital site being cleared and construction getting underway. The insinuation was that the need for such an enormous hospital being built in such a short space of time underscored the seriousness of the outbreak and the potential for widespread population devastation. Retrospect is, of course, a cruel invention yet the rest of the world should have taken more note of what was going on in China and had the USA elected a different president in 2016, it is likely that the situation in China would have been brought into full view for the world to see.

Until the start of 2020, coronaviruses were relatively unknown by the general population. They are a group of viruses that cause mild to moderate upper respiratory tract diseases including the common cold, severe acute respiratory syndrome (SARS) and Middle East respiratory syndrome (MERS). Coronaviruses were discovered in 1967 by the Scottish virologist June Almeida using a new form of imaging, electron microscopy. Having extensively studied the halo of this distinctive virus, she noted the similarity to the sun's outer ring of plasma and the Latin word for crown, corona was chosen. Using electron microscopy, Almeida not only discovered coronaviruses, but she was the first scientist to visualise Rubella (German measles) and her vital immune electron microscopy work was a significant contribution to the diagnosis of both hepatitis B and HIV. Surprisingly, the world has not heard much of her work and her contribution to science and humanity is somewhat under-celebrated.

SARS originated in China in 2002 and is caused by SARS CoV, which had mutated from a coronavirus variant only found in small mammals. There have been two self-limiting outbreaks between 2002 and 2004 where patients contracted the highly contagious virus and suffered a potentially deadly type of pneumonia. No further cases were identified after 2004. In the first pandemic, the infection quickly spread throughout Asia from China and whilst there were a few cases in other countries such as the UK, there was a substantial outbreak in Toronto, Canada. The 2002/3 pandemic was controlled by isolating suspected infected people and screening passengers arriving by air from affected countries for infection signs. In total, there were 8,098 reported SARS cases and 774 deaths, and within the case-fatality rate of 1 in 10 of infected people, it was noted that people older than 65 were at risk, as over half of those who died were in this age group. The second outbreak in 2004 was much smaller and was thought to have arisen from a medical laboratory, the BSL-4 Laboratory in China, where a researcher had come into contact with a SARS virus sample resulting in human-to-human spread as opposed to the initial outbreak caused by animal-to-human transmission. I remember at the time being aware of the SARS outbreaks and was glad that they did not spread more widely. No further SARS cases were identified after 2004.

MERS is a rare yet severe respiratory virus that was transmitted to humans from Saudi Arabian camels in 2012 having, like SARS, also originated in bats. Not surprisingly, it was nicknamed camel-flu. It is caused by MERS-CoV. Similar to SARS, MERS begins with a fever and cough and progresses to pneumonia and

'DYING TO LIVE'

breathing difficulties. It has been relatively confined to the Middle East and outbreaks in South Korea. The death rate is much higher than SARS at around 35% of those infected. Fortunately, there have only been five MERS cases in the UK and the risk of contracting it in the UK remains extremely low. Interestingly, the genetic coding of MERS-CoV is distinctive to SARS and the common cold and, therefore, mutations that could cause a pandemic are less likely.

Other viruses that have mutated and spread to humans include Human Immunodeficiency Virus (HIV), Ebola and swine flu (H1N1). No cases of bird flu (H5N1, H7N9, H5N6, and H5N8) have been found to infect humans. Swine flu was named as it produces symptoms in humans that are similar to that occurring in pigs and was first identified in Mexico in 2009. It is now included in the annual flu vaccine. It spread rapidly from country to country as few younger people had any immunity. Fortunately, the pandemic was less serious than expected as many older people were already immune and most UK cases were, in the end, relatively mild with only a few serious cases. These serious cases that resulted in death occurred mainly in children and young adults with underlying health issues along with pregnant women. Although the pandemic was declared 'over' by the WHO on 10 August 2010, a variant continues to circulate, and the chances are that anyone who has had flu in recent years has suffered from this strain. Interestingly, the swine flu outbreak led to increased preparation for a potential flu pandemic and within my sphere of work, we set about and tested a disaster plan for dealing with this scenario with various levels of shutdown of life and public services depending on severity. Little did I know that these plans would come to bear in 2020.

Although the exact source of the virus has yet to be identified, it is likely that COVID-19 originated at the Huanan Seafood Wholesale Market, a so-called 'wet market' in Wuhan, where live animals such as cats, dogs, rabbits, fish and bats were sold. The market floor is washed continually due to animal slaughtering where blood and bodily fluids mix with melting ice used in meat preservation. It is thought that the common denominator among those who were the first positive cases in Wuhan was animals sold at the Huanan 'wet market'. It is suspected that the virus mutated from an animal coronavirus and was able to jump over to humans due to the environmental conditions in the market. It rapidly spread across the globe to infect Iran and Italy and within a short space of time had infected every continent except Antarctica (until recently). Some of us in the UK even started to worry it would be more serious than SARS or MERS and if the swine flu pandemic plans would be useful.

SARS-CoV-2 is transmitted mainly between people by respiratory secretions including droplets (large particles that are visible) and aerosols (fine mist such as a sneeze) and contact with infected material. Transmission is most effective when people are close together (less than two metres apart). Airborne transmission occurs in places where droplet spread is not contained and where aerosols are generated such as in medical and dental environments. Poor ventilation of indoor spaces also promotes airborne transmission, especially where people are in close proximity within the same room for a long period of time. These routes have resulted in extensive human-to-human transmission within and between countries and although initially reluctant to react, governments and health agencies around the world slowly issued transmission-based precautions for both suspected and confirmed cases for respiratory secretions, blood, faeces and urine.

The enigma of COVID-19 is that the same virus produces wildly differing symptoms and signs of variable severity in different people. Asymptomatic infection is frequent, with many people randomly tested in the UK population later showing antibodies despite no initial outward experience of infection. More frequently, a fever, a new and continuous cough, fatigue, loss of taste (ageusia), loss of smell (anosmia), loss of appetite and shortness of breath occur. There are other symptoms reported including myalgia, sore throat, headache, nasal congestion, diarrhoea, nausea and vomiting and atypical symptoms including delirium and reduced mobility affecting immunocompromised people, sometimes in the absence of a fever. Many cases are likely to be confused with winter-vomiting virus (norovirus) and rotavirus intestinal upsets.

The data suggests that of the people who develop symptoms, 40% have mild problems without low blood oxygen (hypoxia) or pneumonia, 40% have moderate symptoms and pneumonia that is not severe, 15% have a significant level of disease including severe pneumonia, and 5% experience a critical illness form of the disease along with life-threatening complications. This critical illness form is characterised by acute respiratory distress syndrome (ARDS), sepsis, septic shock, cardiac disease, thromboembolic events, such as pulmonary embolisms and multi-organ failure. The major risk factors for severe forms of COVID-19 infection are being older, male, socially deprived and of black and other non-white ethnicities. More recently, it has been found that obesity is also a major risk factor. Conversely, infants generally experience much milder symptoms than adults although a rare presentation of multisystem inflammatory syndrome temporarily associated with COVID-19 in both children and adolescents has been detected. This will require further medical investigation.

Evidence suggests that people who had suffered either mild or severe COVID-19 can, unfortunately, experience prolonged symptoms or can go on to develop long-term complications. Symptoms in tissues that are replaced slowly in the body such as nerve tissue and bones are frequent over the longer term. This is known as Long COVID and is debilitating.

It is worth noting that throughout history, nothing has resulted in greater death among humans than infectious diseases. COVID-19 has demonstrated clearly that humans are vulnerable and the research that has been undertaken to date has the potential to help us avoid future potential pandemics, if used intelligently. This should be on a 'post-it' note on the fridges of all world leaders. Many mass killers remain rife around the world. Malaria (a single-celled parasite which is neither bacterial nor viral) is the best example and is spread by a vector, the humble mosquito. Nothing disturbs a holiday more than the high-pitched buzzing of a mosquito; and once it stops panic sets in as it usually means a bite. Not all areas of the globe with mosquitoes are malarial of course, and whilst the death toll from this disease has dropped substantially over the last 20 years, it still kills half a million people each year. Over the last two millennia, other epidemics have been greater killers, and more importantly on a scale that is unimaginable today,. The Justinianic Plague struck in the sixth century AD and is estimated to have killed as many as 50 million people, around half of the population of the planet at the time. More well-known is the Black Death that was rampant in the fourteenth century and was the same bacterial disease as caused the Justinianic Plague (Yersinia pestis). It is likely that it killed around 200 million people.

Smallpox is caused by the viruses Variola Major and Variola Minor and killed nearly 300 million in the twentieth century, even though the world's first vaccine for this disease was available as early as 1796. Recent calculations of the death toll from the Spanish flu pandemic of 1918-20, which followed the First World War, have increased the estimation of the death toll to 100 million, surpassing that of the war itself, one of the few facts that I found surprising in a history class at school. It also surprised me that this strain of flu infected one third of the globe's population. HIV remains a pandemic to this day and sadly a vaccine has not become available yet with 75 million people infected to date and 32 million having died from this most ghastly disease. The good news is that 14 patients have now been cured of the disease.

Viruses, therefore, have the dubious honour of having killed more humans, at nearly half a billion people, than any other agent including bacteria, parasites and fungal infections. Interestingly, natural disasters such as earthquakes or volcanoes and war do not even come close. Furthermore, natural disasters are constrained by geography as an earthquake will not affect the other side of the globe. Interestingly, bacteria can replicate without infecting cells and although viruses need a host they can remain latent on surfaces unlike bacteria which have a shorter life outwith a suitable host. Viruses are as brilliant at being effective mass killers as they are self-replicators. They do not need to mate to breed. How clever. This puts them at an instant advantage when infecting an animal as they can set about disabling the host defences and then turn the infected cells into breeding machines. Bullets in comparison need to be manufactured, fired and once they hit the target, the metal can only cause mechanical damage. It does not convert the tissue it hits into a factory to manufacture millions of bullets and then fire them at another animal. Most respiratory viruses use the human's natural defences to further their advantage. Coughing and sneezing is one way for a human to try to expel an invader, but in doing so, this offers the perfect route for transmission, right into the face of another human who is likely to breathe in infected air quickly and become the next incubator. No wonder COVID-19 had started to march round the globe.

Until COVID-19, we as the general public knew little about the contagiousness of viruses. We all soon became aware of the 'R' number, the replication number or reproduction number, which is the number of susceptible people that one host can infect. For COVID-19, this has been estimated at 1.5 to 3.5, which is much higher than other viruses, giving COVID-19 yet another advantage: almost guaranteed movement through a population by droplet spread and aerosols using coughing, handshakes and body secretions as the perfect vehicle for transmission. It is reassuring that, for now, at least, no country has been able to successfully develop a biological weapon based on an infectious virus, but it would not take a genius to exploit the R number of COVID-19 in war.

It is worthy of note that, as society has progressed in the developed world, humans are now more likely to die from non-communicable diseases including cardiac disease, cancer and Alzheimer's disease than from contagion. Death rates from infectious diseases had generally dropped by 0.8% each year in the twentieth century. It may seem a tiny step each year, although over a century, this is exceptional progress. This has slowed this century due to population increases over the last 50 years. In this time, the global population has doubled resulting in more opportunities for viruses to infect and spread, especially in areas of higher population density. Increased populations generally utilise more animals in the food chain, producing even more opportunities for animal-to-human transmission. Despite the explosion in population, the decline of infectious diseases is one of the most important factors evidencing the fact that life on Earth has truly improved for the better and continues to improve. COVID-19, however, was the new kid on the block in March in the UK and as a country we were on edge.

COVID-19 has brought into sharp focus two factors. Firstly, the global economy is closely interconnected resulting in the opportunity for infections to be moved to virtually anywhere in the globe within days, and secondly, health and economics are intertwined and any disruption to supply chains can have extensive ramifications. Taking an infection on a trip along with the duty-free facilitates global transmission of viruses before the source patient experiences any symptoms. In spite of the astounding medical advances of the last 50 years, microbes are evolving 40 million times faster than humans and are therefore in the ascendency. To underestimate the potential for viruses to cause a disaster on the scale of the Black Plague is dangerous. It is asking the fox to guard the henhouse. The cost of a pandemic is also literally eye-watering. In 2013, the World Bank estimated that the Spanish flu pandemic would now cost, in real terms, over four trillion dollars, nearly the entire GDP of Japan. Current estimates of the economic damage of the COVID-19 pandemic are three times that at 12 trillion dollars and rising.

The WHO performed brilliantly during the chaos of SARS and MERS but has been criticised over more recent outbreaks of diseases such as the Zika crisis in South America and the Ebola outbreak in Africa. Some experts have called for the organisation to undergo a radical overhaul, particularly as climate change is expanding the transmissibility of diseases by increasing the distance that some animals and insects travel such as Aedes aegypti mosquitoes, which transmit the Zika virus.

The UK's first experience of COVID-19 was when two Chinese nationals who were staying at a hotel in York tested positive at the end of January 2020 after becoming ill. The same day, a plane evacuated UK nationals from China who were transported to a 14-day quarantine hotel in Merseyside. Over the following days, the WHO declared a global health emergency as thousands of new cases of COVID-19 emerged in China, and the US blocked entry to foreign nationals who had travelled to China in the previous fortnight. Cases were rising rapidly and by the end of January, 213 people had died and there were 9,800 infected cases worldwide. Early in February, the first case in Spain was announced and the first COVID-19 death outside China was reported in the Philippines. Three days later, the UK government directed its nationals to leave China if possible. News reports were filled the following day with information about a cruise ship in Southeast Asia. Of the 3,600 people on board, 218 had tested positive and further positive cases were likely.

There was a public outcry when Dr Li Wenliang, who raised the alarm about a cluster of infections which could quickly get out of control, died from COVID-19. It became clear that he had been admonished by the Chinese authorities in early January and was forced to sign a document denouncing his earlier warning as unfounded and an illegal rumour. This was disgraceful and my family and I wondered what other information had been hidden by the Chinese government that could have helped other countries. By the point that the disease was formally named in the middle of February, there were 45,000 cases in China, 393 outside China and 1,113 Chinese nationals had died. The disease was now rampant.

France announced the first COVID-19 death in Europe by mid-February, a Chinese tourist. Egypt confirmed the first case in Africa and within a few days, China announced that it would reassess the trade and consumption of wildlife as a potential cause of the outbreak. It was closing the stable door after the horse had bolted but might prevent a future deadly disease. Later that week, the *Diamond Princess* cruise ship was causing concern as 621 passengers were infected.

The situation started to change suddenly when a case was detected in Iran, but with no known source. Two hours later, Iran publicised two further cases of people who had died and in subsequent days, Iran made public a further two deaths. On the same day, South Korea informed the world that they had taken drastic action following a large number of cases arising in and from the Shincheonji Church of Jesus. Thousands of kindergartens, nursing homes and community centres were temporarily closed. By late February 2020, the virus was moving closer to the UK and with increasing intensity with 150 cases in Italy. Lombardy was locked down, with schools closed, and sporting and cultural events cancelled. This was later extended to cover 50,000 of the population to curb viral spread. President Trump's administration asked Congress for $1.23bn for the US's COVID-19 response even though there were only 35 confirmed cases in the US and no deaths at that point. There were now 61 cases and 12 deaths in Iran. This was of global concern as the route of transmission into Iran remained unknown.

A Brazilian national returning home from Italy became Latin America's first case in late February. Cases in Italy were rising sharply with 800 in total and 14 other European countries were of concern to the WHO. Sub-Saharan Africa announced its first case, the first British victim died on the *Diamond Princess*, the UK confirmed the first case transmitted inside the UK, and the WHO increased the alert to the highest level. Stock markets crashed as a result. Clearly everything was going in the wrong direction, nonetheless, the UK continued as normal for some odd reason and Boris Johnson, the UK Prime Minister, was too busy to attend the first four COBRA meetings about COVID-19.

By the end of February, the US announced the first US COVID-19 death and restricted travel from South Korea and Italy. All travel to Iran was banned and non-US citizens having visited Iran within 14 days were blocked from entering. Boris Johnson finally started attending COBRA meetings, at the fifth meeting, when the outbreak had already started to grip the country. The UK experienced a dramatic increase in cases by 34 to 87 cases in total at the start of March and UK Junior Health Minister Nadine Dorries became the first MP to test positive. More worryingly, six people had died and 373 people had tested positive. Within days the US banned arrivals from Europe except the UK for 30 days, the WHO declared a pandemic and the world stock markets plunged again. Only then did the major governments start to take the potential situation seriously. In the UK, the Chancellor of the Exchequer announced a £12bn emergency support package to help the country overcome the virus.

The US declared a national emergency and $50bn of federal funding was allocated for COVID-19. Many UK sports events were cancelled including the London Marathon. Virtually all football was suspended. By mid-March, Latin America announced restrictions: Venezuela instituted a national quarantine starting the next day, Ecuador and Peru started country lockdowns and Colombia and Costa Rica shut their borders. Brazilian President

Jair Bolsonaro asked his people to demonstrate against his National Congress opponents who wanted to implement restrictions.

Boris Johnson started daily televised briefings in true presidential style, encouraging home working and asked the country to keep away from restaurants and bars to provide breathing space for the NHS. By now, the UK had 1,543 cases and 55 deaths, although it was thought that there were now 10,000 people infected. France enforced a nationwide lockdown blocking all gatherings and only allowing people outside for fresh air. France now had 6,500 positive cases and 140 deaths. The EU prohibited non-EU travellers for 30 days and the UK Chancellor provided one of the largest per-capita financial stimulus emergency state support packages with £330 billion for government-backed loans, £20 billion in tax cuts and grants for companies at risk of failing. Only on 18 March, did the UK government finally close schools in England and the administrations in Wales, Northern Ireland and Scotland followed suit. By then, many more people had become infected and had this measure been put in place earlier, fewer serious cases and deaths would have resulted in the first wave.

China reported zero new cases on 19 March, a key step. It was thought by experts that this would need to continue for 14 days for the outbreak to be declared over. The statement was slightly incorrect as 34 new cases were found among people arriving in China. The following day, saw the UK plan lockdown and the furlough scheme was announced to cover up to 80% of wages during the lay off period to keep people in jobs. The UK lockdown was tightened on 23 March when Boris Johnson announced in a TV address that people should only leave their house to purchase food, exercise for one hour per day or to travel to work if there was no possibility of working from home. Now the world had seen 270,000 cases and 11,000 deaths. Quite shocking. It was made public that the Tokyo Olympics set for August were likely to be postponed with several countries confirming their athletes would not be allowed to travel. The next day, the Royal Family had its first case with Prince Charles testing positive and, in the US, a $2trn package to help businesses and citizens was announced. This included $1,200 for each American earning up to $75,000, $100bn for healthcare, $58bn for the airline industry and $2,400 per month for up to four months for the unemployed. There was also $500bn for industry loans to corporations, cities and states. India entered a 21-day lockdown even though the country had only reported 536 cases and in Brazil, President Jair Bolsonaro was unhappy with the COVID-19 safety measures being implemented by local government. The world stood back and said nothing of his actions; he should have been held to account.

A virtual summit of the G20 world leaders took place at the end of March to discuss the COVID-19 crisis at which King Salman of Saudi Arabia asked the world's richest countries to 'extend a helping hand to developing countries'. The UK population clapped, cheered, and rang bells at 8pm every Thursday evening to thank the NHS workers for their input to the pandemic which unified the country. The Chancellor announced a further financial stimulus for self-employed workers, covering 80% of average profits for those earning less than £50,000. The next day, Boris Johnson and Health Secretary Matt Hancock tested positive for COVID-19 and Hungarian Prime Minister Viktor Orbán commented publicly that the pandemic has demonstrated EU 'weaknesses'. At a rally on 28 March, European Commission President Ursula von der Leyen said the EU 'looked into the abyss' early in the pandemic and now had the opportunity for reinvention. French President Emmanuel Macron pleaded for European solidarity, saying, 'I don't want a selfish and divided Europe'. Belgium extended the lockdown measures until mid-April. When the UK Chief Medical Officer, Chris Whitty, started self-isolation due to COVID-19 symptoms, it was now clear that anyone could contract the virus.

The European Commission declared that the EU's next seven-year budget will be revised, and the US, after recording nearly

140,000 cases, the highest number worldwide, confirmed social distancing measures would continue until 30 April. On 30 March, Viktor Orbán was given absolute power by the Hungarian Parliament to rule by decree, impose a non-time-limited state of emergency and suspend parliament. The same day, the UK Foreign Secretary provided £75 million funding to repatriate up to 300,000 British nationals stuck in countries with closed borders. Sadly, on 31 March, Spain, along with the US and Italy, were surpassing China's coronavirus case total, reporting 85,000 cases and 8,000 deaths. Ethiopia postponed parliamentary and presidential elections in August and the White House estimated there would be 100,000 to 240,000 deaths from COVID-19 in 2020, even if current social distancing was maintained.

By the end of March, there had been a total of 856,955 cases in the world and 37,140 deaths. I did not want to be a case and definitely did not want to be in the fatal statistics, but this was now well beyond my control.

———————

CHAPTER 3

_____

Who am I?

WHO AM I? This is a question I have asked myself regularly in the time since I became unwell. It may seem a bit strange to you reading this book but a critical illness provides an ideal opportunity to examine your psyche in great detail. This is because of the time available to think and because at times your life flashes before you so the years are somehow compressed into the space of a few minutes. This is a frightening experience. Normally I wouldn't spend time dwelling on past actions and experiences, that is not to say that I am heartless with no concern for those around me or those with whom I interact. It is the opposite. I worry about the effect my actions have on others, and particularly if I have inadvertently caused offence. Even when driving, I prefer to smile at the selfish driver rather than remonstrate. Before COVID-19, I saw my roles to be a husband, a father, an NHS consultant, a professorial colleague and a friend. COVID-19 showed me that another descriptor should be added, that of being a friend to many colleagues within my profession.

I was born in October 1970 as the third son to my wonderful parents, Colin and Allison. As the youngest son, I followed in the footsteps of my two older brothers, John and Callum. John was academically brilliant and was on track to study medicine from an early age. Callum worked hard and although he didn't have a clear career path, studying law was a natural choice for him. Neither of my older brothers caused our parents any worry and provided them with many opportunities to celebrate success at school and in other areas of childhood. I was the rebel, not in a caustic sense, I just didn't see the point in working at school as it was dictatorial, and I knew I was never going to beat my brothers either academically or outwith school. This frustrated my parents who couldn't understand why I didn't make the best use of the chances they had provided. Looking back, I guess I could have put in a little more effort, not just enough to pass the key exams as I did but to pass them more comfortably.

As brothers, we looked after each other whether it be at school or in the Scouts, where we all went through various groups and had many positive experiences. This was a very formative period for all three of us and we continue to keep in touch with the friends we all made 40 years ago. During the school holidays, our parents would send us off to Scout camp; they never truly discovered what we got up to. Some activities only now grace the conversations when we meet around the dinner table. We learned respect for self, others and possessions very clearly. Whilst we did some crazy things when camping, abseiling, canoeing, skiing, climbing and hill-walking, we and those around us ensured that everyone remained safe.

I decided around age 15 that my career lay in dentistry which was the occupation of our favourite uncle who, along with his wife and children, spent a lot of time with us and helped us in many ways. I felt my uncle had made the ideal lifestyle for himself and his family. He was his own boss, only worked from nine to five, had an amazing house and dental practice, enjoyed relatively exotic holidays, and always had a decent car. At one point, he had a Ford Granada which made a magnificent noise and looked just the part for a 1970s police drama. I had decided that following in his footsteps would be sensible as I could run my own race in life. I wouldn't need to compete with my brothers. I duly worked out the bare minimum to study dentistry as a career and did the rounds of interviews to enter university. Sadly, I was too young by ten days to begin a course as a result of an arbitrary threshold and therefore had to study a sixth year at school.

Whilst academically this was a waste of time, I made the most of the year in broadening friendships. It was a good time. I chose to study biology, chemistry and physics, the latter since it clashed with the biology course and I would miss half the classes. I was delighted when I was summoned to see the rector having recorded the lowest ever mark in the school in a mock A-level exam. This had no effect on me, and I passed the A-level exam with one evening's revision. I already had six Scottish Higher passes from the year before and an unconditional offer for entry to university, so I saw no need to work hard. How I would love to meet the deputy head from primary school who told my parents that 'he didn't think I would amount to much in life'. I wonder if he would now agree the system might have been part of the problem as well as my 'just enough' approach to learning as a child.

At university, my life opened up. I loved university life and although I stayed at home, there was much to enjoy both on campus and through the 'hidden curriculum'. I made some more lifelong friendships and although I didn't excel in anatomy, physiology and chemistry, I knew what would be needed to pass each key exam. Indeed, I didn't fail any exam at university and the only scare I had was on seeing the results for biochemistry in year one, where I had apparently failed. On asking the senior lecturer where I had gone wrong, he identified an addition error and somehow the marks for me and a classmate with the same surname had been transposed. Naturally I was relieved. Poor Johnny was very unhappy at being told that he now had a resit. Sadly my father died suddenly midway through year two and rather than leaving home for a flat, I elected to stick around and help my mother. I had had a variety of jobs during the holidays and did my best to look after the practical aspects of running the family home since both my older brothers had left home.

I enjoyed the clinical subjects of dentistry more and found I was a natural at orthodontics. Whether it was the inspiring academic staff or the female dental nurses that enthused me is left to the reader to decide. I decided in year four that my career lay in orthodontics and worked out that there would be many more years of postgraduate study to do.

Having graduated, I did my first postgraduate year as a general dentist in a small market town and got married during the year. My boss worked at the dental school where I had studied and I knew him well. It didn't take him long to explain that I should pursue my career and he let me know I would be frustrated as a general dentist. It was good advice. I subsequently went to work in a provincial hospital in north-west England. There was no interview, I just sent a letter of application and was asked to turn up on a specific date. I applied for this post as it had a mix of oral surgery and orthodontics and I decided it would be better to try out the specialty before studying any further. This was a fabulous job and involved being on-call for all sorts of dental emergencies, facial injuries and head and neck trauma. My first weekend on-call involved dealing with a road traffic accident victim who we had to take to the operating theatre to remove masses of shattered windscreen glass embedded in his face and scalp. I wondered how my undergraduate teachers had prepared me for this moment but remembered one professor telling me that while the hands work, the brain should learn. There was the mix of facial trauma, abscesses, cancer, all sorts of swellings and teeth of varying shapes and sizes to attend to day and night. The consultant orthodontist, Mr Bray, showed me the basics of my future speciality and let me learn much more by providing an immersion in my intended speciality.

I moved back to Glasgow and for the next two and a half years I worked in my alma mater doing a range of dental and surgical specialities whilst being part of the on-call rota for surgery at night and weekends for the north half of the city. Glasgow is a very friendly place by day but is known for inter-personal trauma fuelled by alcohol at night. It would become almost routine to be operating to repair fractured jaws and facial bones. The team I worked with encouraged me to pursue my career and by the end of this time, I had passed both parts of my fellowship examination which was the gatekeeper to becoming a specialist. I now had another series of letters after my name and my mother was delighted. Finally, I was able to demonstrate to her that she did not need to worry about me.

I was now ready to apply for a speciality training post in orthodontics. I went on the merry-go-round with the other applicants and travelled the UK for interviews in various interesting places. I was successful at my fifth interview and was ecstatic. It was time to move to a new house again, this time in the east of Scotland. I had not spent any real time in Dundee or Perth before this juncture; and now I was to spend several years in and around both cities. I remember going to Dundee University for an interview and recall the dental hospital being close to the city. Later, I went to Dundee for an annual inter-university 'Field Day', which was meant to involve sport, but the only 'sport' that was ever contested seemed to be alcohol. Times have changed for the better and these inter-university drinking days are now held on Fridays to protect the public.

Moving to the east of Scotland was to be an important step in my life and energised my career. My wife Marie and I bought a house in Blairgowrie, a small provincial market town in the hinterland of Perth and Dundee. It meant that I would need to commute but this was hardly a punishment since a traffic jam consisted of two tractors and a cyclist! By day, I worked in a clinic learning the skills of my chosen field under the tutelage of four consultants and in the evening, I studied the knowledge aspects. I enrolled for a master's degree by research under the supervision of one of my academic supervisors, later to become a professor of craniofacial development and a lifelong academic colleague as well as a friend.

As my clinical programme developed, Marie became pregnant and gave birth to our son Colin. I was now a father as well and this was an amazing time in my life. I remember the day he was born clearly. I finished work at the hospital, walked across the car park just in time for the Caesarean section to begin. Within an hour, I had become a father and the midwife gave me my son, Colin, wrapped in a blanket. I was slightly shocked and wondered where the instruction manual, training course and responsibility payment was. Joking aside, it did give me a wake-up call that I had an additional responsibility and just as when my father had died, I needed to grow up a little further. I, therefore, gathered the portfolio material ready for my speciality examination; I was successful at my first attempt and was ready to be registered as a specialist.

I could now focus on my master's degree project, which was investigating the cranial and facial shape of parents whose children were born with a cleft, using X-rays. I enjoyed the discovery aspect of research and spent many hours in the library and at home using the fledgling internet to identify appropriate information and evidence to help me write my thesis and conduct my research project. Whilst undertaking my research, I published other scientific papers, some of which, surprisingly, remain relevant today. As my research developed, I was given the opportunity to present the early results at various conferences. I felt that I was starting to be part of the wider research 'machine'. I was asked by the professor and head of department to give him the results section of my thesis to evaluate. I duly obliged even though it was not in a finished state. Having looked at it, he gave me the next weekend to decide if I wanted to take material out to submit for a master's degree or to continue on with my research and submit a thesis for a PhD.

By Monday, it was clear to me that having gone this far, the PhD was worth the additional work. Over the next year, my research broadened and deepened to include additional experimental work. Unfortunately, my 'stipendiary' contract was coming to an end and I had to look for another job to support my young family.

I was fortunate to be offered a promotion to a pre-consultant post in the west of Scotland, which meant moving house again and further disruption to family life. Little did Marie or I know that she was pregnant again although sadly she was to lose the baby during the pregnancy. It was a devastating time for all of the family and my son had to deal with the loss of a potential sibling at a very young age. It was a sad time in my life and I often wonder what may have been.

As my new job developed, I set the date for submission of my PhD thesis working by day as an orthodontist and in the evenings, weekends and nights, and sometimes overnight, on my thesis. I duly submitted the thesis and a few months later successfully defended it. I could now be an independent researcher and was delighted to graduate for the fourth time. As my pre-consultant post rolled on, I became eligible to sit the next professional exam. Unlike earlier exams, there were only six candidates for this exam and the examiners and candidates were familiar with each other. Unfortunately, the other candidates and I were not informed that the portfolio section was changed two weeks before the exam and unfortunately, the other candidates and I did not pass. It was the first exam I had failed in my life. It was a long drive back from Cardiff having been unsuccessful. Whilst this was brutally disappointing at the time, it has helped me in my subsequent professional career to help others through exam failures and difficult periods.

Six months later, I re-sat the single section I had failed, and passed. I didn't bother with this graduation, which would have been my fifth. After that, I was interviewed for a consultant post in the east of Scotland and again a further house move was on the cards. This would be the dream job for life, so we chose to buy a slightly run-down house and spent a great deal of energy renovating it. Within two years, Marie admitted to having an affair and left. I filed for a legal separation to protect the rights of my son and in time the divorce was finalised.

I continued to work as a consultant and loved the work. I was keen to develop the services we ran for patients with facial clefts to mirror my major research interest and also the facial deformity service. The cleft service in most countries is organised around the various surgical procedures that children with clefts require. An initial surgery to close a lip cleft is undertaken at three months and a cleft of the palate is repaired at nine months. If there is a gum cleft, this is repaired at nine to twelve years and any mismatch in the jaws is treated around age 18 to 20.

Orthodontic input and treatment are required around all these surgical procedures and orthodontic-led research has helped refine the timing and types of initial surgeries that are undertaken so that the amount of scarring-related deformity has reduced, to the benefit of the child, parents, NHS and worldwide health systems. Many of the patients and families I have treated over 20-plus years I now know well, and some have gone onto have their own children, some with clefts who I am now treating. It is rewarding to work as part of a multi-disciplinary team that includes speech and language therapists, audiologists, paediatricians, geneticists and, of course, surgeons, who take the lead.

I have also enjoyed being part of the facial deformity service which is an equal undertaking to being part of the cleft service and, over the years, our team has treated over a thousand patients with a combination of orthodontic braces and major corrective jaw surgery. I spend considerable amounts of time with patients prior to surgery preparing them for, in many cases, the first major operation they have experienced. As with the cleft service, the surgeon is usually sovereign. One of the surgeons, Sam, who has a personality akin to Sir Lancelot Spratt from the Carry On films, gives me my place during clinics whilst the other, Timothy, more of a gentle giant, keeps telling me that I am the boss in clinic. I feel like a double agent and the go-between since most surgeons want to be the alpha; communication between them is perfunctory.

It surprises me that despite spending considerable amounts of time preparing patients for a major operation, that they rarely overestimate how they will feel on waking up after surgery. In particular, young men are usually the least sensible in their preparation for surgery and some have an alcohol-fuelled night out the weekend before surgery meaning after surgery their liver is dealing with alcohol as well as the anaesthetic drugs resulting in a longer recovery period post-op. Many mothers of young men going through this stage seem to enjoy having their 'baby' back and relish having to care for their son again. Older men who have a long-term partner and, women of all ages, in my experience, prepare more sensibly and are much more independent.

The constant in the team is the laboratory staff who, when in any discussion about individual cases, have the wisdom of Solomon. Our team has expanded and now treats an increasing number of patients from other areas of Scotland; and as a surgical and orthodontic team we go to other areas each month for clinics. This is a great experience where I usually travel with my good friends Kunal and Sam. Whilst away, we usually have dinner together, a glass or two of wine and a small whisky nightcap. As you can imagine, we also put the world to rights.

After four years on my own as a single parent, I decided that the time was right to look for love again. Colin was becoming older, and his horizons were expanding. I met the wonderful Amanda and we instantly hit it off. We talked endlessly about how we would plan our future together and what we both wanted from life and each other. Whilst I had only one child, Colin, Amanda had three slightly older children – Jonathan, Anna and Alexander – who had different needs and we were conscious that the joining of two families of unequal size would have to be done carefully to cater for each of the children's needs, wants and wishes. We took things slowly at first and gradually introduced the children to each other and over the next year, went on holiday a few times as a large unit.

As the years rolled on, we frequently took Anna's friend Georgie with us on holiday (and her parents frequently took Anna). During a holiday in Spain, I remember parking a hired people carrier in a small town. After all the family had got out onto the pavement, an elderly Spanish man came over and shook my hand. My Spanish is at the level of the tourist while Amanda is schooled in many languages and explained to me that the gentleman was congratulating me on my large family and that I must be a taurus (raging bull) in the bedroom. I was somewhat delighted, for although I only had one biological child, to the outward eye, it appeared that the rest of the now adolescent children were, including Anna's friend Georgie, together!

We set about the difficult question of moving as neither of our houses was suitable for a large family. We decided to build a new house somewhere in the middle. We looked for plots of land for many months and eventually found an ideal plot in a small development of houses in a rural area. Neither of us had done such a project before but it was exciting. Whilst we did not do any of the serious building work, we were actively involved in every aspect of the project and spent considerable time ensuring all work was done to the highest standard. We built a lovely house and have been very proud of our achievement even though our main contractor vanished when a major building fault appeared in the part-completed garage - that of water ingress. I am no builder but I learned quickly that re-doing building work is expensive and with such a fault, repair is trial and error. Even a surveyor couldn't identify the source of the problem. We set about dealing with this problem from top down and in the end, with the tutelage of YouTube and other internet sites, re-laid the garage floor, coated the walls with a waterproofing tanking material to make it watertight and finished the rest of the building. It is now some structure and will be our nuclear bunker if needed. It might even challenge the next ice age. Whereas Amanda would not want to deal with the stress of building ever again, I am tempted from time-to-time and indulge myself by watching *Grand Designs*.

We settled into a routine in our new home and time passed. The children finished school and in two cases university. Suddenly they were all adults. We now had time to concentrate on each other and Amanda proposed that we should get married. This was always on the cards. We had planned to celebrate our wedding in the finished house and garden. Due to some issues with the landscaper, part of the garden remains unfinished to this very day. We, therefore, set a date for the wedding in a hotel and celebrated our special day with many of our family and close friends. We were finally legal even though many people had assumed that we had already tied the knot secretly.

Alongside my clinical career, I continued with academic pursuits, training the next generation of orthodontists and developing my NHS managerial experience. I continued to explore research areas of interest and publish papers on a regular basis. As time passed, I was asked to become involved in supervising postgraduate research students, which provided a new focus. As I had always enjoyed teaching, I relished the opportunity to become Training Programme Director in our region and chair various assessment panels, a role that I have only recently given up due to the time commitment involved.

Supervising research students involves different skills and is less of a master-apprentice model and more of a guiding-hand approach to investigate specific areas without having the answer to the question, just the skills to know how to carry out the investigation. Whether it be for a master's degree or a PhD, I have had the opportunity to work with some very gifted students who have gone on to become solid researchers in their own units. In time, I hope several will become professors and heads of department. I encourage each research student to publish as much as they can from their thesis as publishing their findings in the public domain allows others in the areas of interest to best use the findings and knowledge to the best use. Therefore, with the help of this group of students, I surpassed my career goal of

50 papers fairly quickly and by age 46, I had over 100 papers to my name. I am proud to be associated with our research laboratory that has a consistent track record of winning research funding, working with dedicated research students and producing high quality outputs, which are widely regarded within our university and beyond. Indeed, our laboratory is designated by the WHO for craniofacial and population oral health research.

My contribution was rewarded by promotion from senior lecturer to reader to professor in the space of two years, all on an honorary basis since the NHS was my employer. It was truly delightful to be asked to come to see the Dean at age 46 to be informed that Senate had unanimously approved my promotion to professorial status and we became the only dental school in the UK with three professors in orthodontics. As a team of three, we continue to cross-collaborate with each other along with many other institutions in the UK and worldwide on a variety of projects. I can still remember phoning my mother to let her know that I was now a professor. She had expected there to be a ceremony and was surprised to discover that it was a mere formality of a confirmatory letter from the University Secretary. Around the same time, the opportunity to become further involved in NHS management of our dental hospital became available with the retiral of a senior colleague and I put myself forwards for the new position of Clinical Director. This was to become the biggest challenge of my clinical career, being jointly responsible for a building and service with a £10 million annual budget and 150 direct employees - the biggest out-patient hospital in the region.

I would now work more closely with university colleagues in the building to ensure our clinical teaching facilities and opportunities were as good as they could be for our 400 undergraduate and postgraduate students, and work with more senior NHS colleagues further up the food chain in the surgical directorate. I had to learn many new skills and fast. Reading large budget statements is tricky and they have to be checked for errors. Why should one of our 25 budgets be charged for another unit's drugs or equipment? Being the boss means that there is a constant stream of HR enquiries, most genuine, of course, but some needing the 'rule-book' to be consulted and applied fairly. It has been a pleasure to be allowed to help dedicated colleagues through times both good and tricky as I would like the same in reverse. Some people do surprise and sadly they do some stupid things in their private life that require disciplinary intervention and, in some cases, suspension or dismissal. Again, the judgement of Solomon is required for these occasions; once rumours start moving round a large building, the managers are usually blamed, if only for doing their job. One of the challenges of being a senior manager is the volume of documents that need to be read as everyone expects the boss to have all the answers. Sitting in multiple meetings each day, week after week, can test the patience of a saint. My approach is to make the most of working with people no matter how boring the subject under discussion.

This all came to an abrupt stop on 31 March 2020 when I contracted COVID-19, and I went from being a parent, husband, colleague, researcher, manager and friend to a rapidly dying patient, in Ninewells Hospital and Medical School, Dundee.

———————————

CHAPTER 4

Dead or Alive

THE FIRST DAY of April 2020 was no April Fools' Day. I was now at death's door. I had not been alone in being relatively relaxed about deteriorating and feeling that I was dying before being anaesthetised. I would later discover that this would happen to other patients as well. The doctors call it 'happily hypoxic' but it was no laughing matter. Apparently one of the unusual facts about severe COVID-19 is the sensation of a silent death with a calmness and serenity that is unlike death from many other diseases. There is no restlessness as the patient gently slips away into unconsciousness and stops breathing. I had not felt 'happily hypoxic' at any point though.

I did not know what was to come next or indeed how much destruction the COVID-19 virus was to cause to my body. I was now reliant on those caring for me for survival and had entrusted my body and mind to their expertise, whilst I wanted God to take care of my soul. The doctors' sagacity and sangfroid in Ninewells Hospital were beyond doubt. I had no power over any decisions and knew as I came into hospital that I had surrendered my dignity and now I had surrendered all control. Asking to be put on CPAP was the biggest decision of my life and I had no idea what lay ahead. As I went to sleep, I hoped CPAP would give my lungs a chance to repair so that I would survive. Surprisingly, I hadn't realised at this point that I would not need to be anaesthetised to be put on CPAP. I have been involved in jaw surgery for patients with obstructive sleep apnoea where the throat collapses at night and the oxygen saturation level drops significantly. We regularly ask patients to bring their CPAP equipment to clinic and check that it fits their jaws, particularly if they are considering corrective jaw surgery for significant jaw mismatches. On some occasions, it is clear that the obstructive sleep apnoea is due in part to the mismatch in jaw size and position, but in other cases, the real issue is because of obesity, poor mask-fitting technique or lack of persistence with the CPAP machine.

I was oblivious to the news. I was anaesthetised and must have been extremely unwell not to realise that I was being prepared for something much more invasive and I am sure the medical team were being very kind to me by not mentioning that CPAP, even with a helmet or any other adjuncts to improve oxygenation of my blood, would be useless due to the severity of my condition. I had not realised at this point that I was now suffering from COVID-19 related pneumonia. Amanda and the close family knew which hospital I was in, but they had no idea where I was in the hospital or what was going on. Like me, I don't think they knew how seriously ill I was at this point. Indeed, nobody, the medical staff included, knew how unwell I was to become. It was now all about survival, but I was not able to participate in this.

As part of my clinical work, I have been involved in many surgical operations and know that the anaesthetic and indeed the anaesthetist do not get the credit they deserve. After all, the patient comes to hospital for an operation, not for an anaesthetic says the time-old saying. I did come for the anaesthetic on this occasion; to be put on to a ventilator and needed to be anaesthetised. The anaesthetist/ICU doctors were not going to be able to sit back and relax and do the crossword while everything else was being taken care of by an oft grumpy surgeon who is convinced that they are the 'top dog' in the operating theatre. In this case, they were going to do everything from the point of the anaesthetic onwards.

The key in any emergency situation is 'access' to the lungs and into a good-sized vein - and an arterial line. Other access would be needed once I was stabilised. As access to a vein had already been gained by inserting a cannula into a vein in my left arm, the next procedure was to gain access to my lungs for the ventilator. This is called intubation and involved placing a plastic endo-tracheal (through the windpipe) ventilator tube through my mouth and down into my lungs to establish and maintain an adequate airway. This allows the ventilator to provide an ample exchange of oxygen and carbon dioxide through a humidified and heated circuit. It is important that the oxygen is humidified to prevent the internal workings of the lungs from drying out and sticking; and the incoming air to be heated to body temperature.

I was placed onto a portable ventilator in the high dependency unit and transferred to the additional intensive care unit that had been set up in the operating theatre suite recovery area (ICU2) alongside multiple other patients and although this was early in the first UK wave of COVID-19, the medical team had already gained a great deal of experience of COVID-19 patients requiring ventilation. I knew as I went to sleep that I was in some of the safest hands in the country. Once in the ICU2 area, I was established on an ICU ventilator. There was more work for the team to do, though.

The next access is an arterial line or an A-line, which is more complex due to the anatomical depth of arteries compared to veins. A thin plastic catheter tube was inserted into the radial artery in my left wrist and was connected to the blood pressure, pulse and ECG monitor. Through some clever wizardry, it allows real-time measurement of blood pressure and facilitates blood gas measurement for the assessment of oxygen and carbon dioxide in the blood to determine the efficiency of the lungs, without the need to frequently access an artery. I remember as a junior the difficulty in accessing arterial blood in times of crisis for the measurement of blood gases. The monitor is part of a sophisticated monitoring system displaying the body's key functions showing waveforms, numbers and audible alarms. To accompany the recording system, three ECG 'dots' had been placed at various points across my chest in HDU and an oxygen saturation probe attached to a finger and all connected to the monitor with leads. The medical and nursing teams are hugely skilled at keeping an eye on the ICU monitor. It almost becomes second knowledge to them to know what is normal and abnormal for heart rate, blood pressure, body temperature, breathing rate and oxygen saturation while almost a glance and their sixth sense can determine when the patient is about to deteriorate without waiting for the monitor to sound an alarm. A central venous line was also inserted in my right jugular vein in my neck for greater and more reliable venous access than the small cannula in the back of my hand used to anaesthetise me. This is used for anaesthetic agents, fluids, electrolytes, insulin and other drugs, as well as to monitor central venous pressure.

My body was in a state of inflammation due to the pneumonia. This made my blood vessels 'leaky' with fluid escaping into the surrounding tissues resulting in generalised swelling. As a result, vasopressor drugs were required for cardiovascular support to maintain the tone of the blood vessels and keep my blood pressure up for blood to flow to and from the vital organs. There were various clots occurring throughout my body as well. With my respiratory system needing ventilator support and my kidneys requiring dialysis and my neurological system suffering from brain dysfunction due to the sedation drugs and infection (septic encephalopathy), I was now in multi-organ failure.

The main purpose of the ventilator is to push oxygen into the lungs, whilst keeping the lungs, and in particular the alveolar sacs at the periphery of the lungs where most gas exchange takes place, inflated. Gases are removed from the lungs as the ventilator deflates, but still contains a greater amount of carbon dioxide and other gas by-products than atmospheric air. At this point in treatment, the ventilator was doing all the work of breathing for me. The final piece of the ventilator kit is a suction catheter which is a long flexible tube which passes down inside the endotracheal tube. This allows secretions (mainly mucous) to be sucked up and removed, as when in respiratory failure and being paralysed on a ventilator, the normal lung clearance mechanisms do not adequately function. The catheter is attached to a suction canister and a negative pressure suction tube on the wall. Regular suction is used to prevent 'plugging' and any other areas of collapse. Temperature regulation is an important consideration in ICU and especially so in my case as before going into hospital my temperature regulation was haywire. Heating and cooling blankets above and below are sometimes used to help regulate body temperature but at least I did not need these.

A nasogastric tube was inserted through my nose and down into my stomach for feeding, secured by tape to my cheek. I didn't know it at the time but Arianne, the dietician, came to see me frequently to determine my calorie requirements and prescribed the required amount of liquid feed to be administered continuously through the nasogastric tube. The nasogastric tube is also used for the delivery of certain medications which are needed to be given through the gut. Drugs are administered using a syringe while liquid feed is delivered by a pump which can slowly deliver the feed over many hours and can signal any problem with feeding through an alarm.

A catheter had been inserted in HDU into my bladder to deal with urine and a flexi-seal at the other end for faeces. I was hooked up to various machines to continuously monitor my pulse, blood pressure and oxygen saturation level. I was initially nursed on my back (the supine position) but then moved to the prone position known as being 'proned'. This helps the blood maintain an adequate level of oxygenation by improving lung volume and redistribution of oxygenation throughout the lungs and recruitment of the sections of lung in the back. This technique also results in a more even spread of blood oxygenation through-out the lung tissues as the lungs act like a sponge in a pneumonia situation and become 'soggy'. In essence, being proned results in better ventilation. It also stops the weight of the front of the chest crushing the lungs thus causing further damage.

Being proned constantly is not possible so the nursing staff would be required to turn me and the other ventilated patients from prone to supine periodically, although my head would be turned every four hours and arms stretched at the same time. This is normally a challenging task with all the lines and monitoring equipment. The task becomes inordinately more difficult with a COVID-19 patient on a ventilator and medical / nursing staff having to wear full personal protective equipment. At this point, the infection control doctors had advised everyone coming into contact with COVID-19 patients to double glove for precaution as the infectivity of the virus was not known. Overshoes were also worn in some hospitals as a further precaution. Specific areas for 'donning' and 'doffing' PPE have to be organised as well as PPE supplies. I had known in the weeks leading up to falling ill that the supplies of PPE were, at this point challenging, but fortunately knew that ICU had been prioritised. Had I known anything about my condition, I would have advised the nursing staff to take every precaution with me as I had conceded to myself in the preceding days that somehow I had a high viral load and was inevitably highly infectious at this point. It would horrify me to think that I might have potentially infected anyone, far less the team that had been my lifeline. What if I had infected anyone and they had died? I would not want to be responsible for such a tragedy having witnessed the virus rip through communities and families on the TV in the weeks prior to falling ill.

Amanda phoned the hospital to discover where I was. She was shocked to discover that I was in ICU. Thankfully, the team took great care to explain to her that I had been involved in part of the decision and knew that being on a ventilator was the best course of action. There was also a degree of positivity on day one in ICU as I had been given a high dose of steroids to calm my immune system and this appeared to be having a beneficial effect. Amanda was relieved that this was good news, at last.

The number of positive cases in the world reached a million the next day (2 April 2020) and I was one of them. Unaware of what was happening to me, I had no idea that the hospital had an excellent critical care rehabilitation programme which starts on day one in ICU. While the NHS often comes under criticism from the public, most people are generally unaware of what goes on behind the scenes. The general public can only comment on the services and staff they come into contact with and when things do not go their way, they vent their frustration and sometimes their anger. I had little understanding of the 'behind the scenes' activity that takes place in the intensive care units up and down the country but had enough understanding from my time working in oral surgery as well as oral and maxillofacial surgery as a junior that a full multi-disciplinary team looks after each patient and focuses on their specific needs. I also knew that the nursing ratio was much higher than on a normal ward to cope with the intensity of the care that is delivered.

I had no reason to doubt that all patients would receive anything but the best care in the hospital I worked in but as my patients rarely go to ICU, I was oblivious to the extent of the team who would now be caring for me. I later discovered that the critical care team would be one of the most functional teams I would ever meet, and little did I know they all know each other's roles clearly and share learning on a 'no question is too stupid to ask' basis. Their philosophy of care was simple. The end starts at the beginning and evidence-based care is delivered on an empathetic basis with the patient and family consulted at every stage. Had I known what was going on, I would have been content to know that the staff would contact Amanda with an update on my condition twice per day. However, my condition had deteriorated, and I was now struggling to fight the sepsis in my lungs, my kidneys had failed completely and multi-organ failure was not improving. Amanda was given this bad news. Callum felt it was better to protect our elderly mum from the difficult news that I was on a ventilator and having discussed this with John, they agreed that it would be better to let Mum know that I was receiving 'extra oxygen'.

Casey, one of the critical care physiotherapists, had been to see me on my first day in ICU. I have no recollection of meeting her. She undertook a full assessment of my physical needs and with her team leader, Sophie, they devised a programme to keep my limbs, joints and muscles working periodically each day in the hope that I might recover. It must have been strange for so many of the team to meet me in a coma and not have met me in a conscious state prior to coming into hospital. Building a relationship with, to all intents, a body which is not accompanied by a functioning mind, must be challenging to say the least. How would they know what my likes and dislikes were, my personality or indeed what my voice sounded like? At this point in the first COVID-19 wave, my mother later told me the news was continually depressing with each bulletin starting with an announcement on the number of new cases and the number of deaths. Somehow, the ICU staff had to maintain hope for every patient no matter how ill each patient was and deal with the background of working in the area of the hospital containing the patients who were most seriously ill. Death is a frequent occurrence in ICU as a result and COVID-19 must have compounded the normal sadness of patients dying from strokes, cardiac events, major trauma and so on. It must have been a horrendous time for the staff. Looking back now, I wonder who was caring for the critical care team.

I had assumed when asking to be put on CPAP, perhaps rather naively, that CPAP or even a ventilator would give my lungs time to rest as it would mechanically oxygenate my blood and as a result, my immune system would deal with the pneumonia. How wrong I was. Whilst the intensive care doctors continued to ensure my lungs were oxygenated, the amount of pneumonia was life-threatening. Essentially, my lungs were filled with fluid and secretions as my body mounted its response to the COVID-19 infection over the next few days. The doctors told Amanda that I was not only suffering from a severe COVID-19 infection, but my own body was mounting such a huge immune response that I was in greater jeopardy now. The daily updates were becoming more stressful for all concerned.

This over-exaggerated immune response is known as a cytokine storm or hypercytokinemia, where my body released, or in fact, unleashed, a ferocious response of cascading exaggerated inflammatory signalling molecules but, in doing so, caused a great deal of damage to the tissues infected by COVID-19, in this case principally the lungs but other areas of the body as well. There are a multitude of cytokines in the body, and they have a number of different functions. Some are for the recruitment of other cells involved in immunity and others produce antibodies or are part of the cell signalling pathways for communication and, in particular, pain. In relation to the blood system, there are cytokines that assist with blood clotting, a well-known cascade of factors along with those involved in inflammation, which led to the blood vessels becoming even more leaky causing more swelling. Interestingly, there is another group of cytokines that help calm down the inflammatory response, but these must not have been working particularly well as by now, I was exhibiting a significant amount of general swelling, known as oedema and was ballooning in size. Along with this, the doctors were aware of overwhelming inflammation, hyperferritinaemia (a marker of iron overload in the blood), haemodynamic instability (inability to move blood round the body normally) and were trying to manage my multiple organ failure. Very low blood pressure and increased blood clotting edoccurred, compounding the damage to organs and tissues. My heart did not pump as well as it would normally. As a result, the cytokine storm affected multiple organ systems, potentially leading to organ failure and potential death was on the cards. My lungs were now suffering from Acute Respiratory Distress Syndrome (ARDS). Death resulting from ARDS occurs in around 50% of patients, whilst for others, some damage may be permanent through scarring meaning that oxygenation is not as good as it was beforehand. It was, therefore, unknown that if I survived would any damage be permanent or repairable since no previous information on COVID-19 was available to the doctors. I was now critically ill and closer to death than I would ever want to be. Amanda was horrified at what was happening, and helpless at the same time.

Despite the ICU doctors knowing what was happening to me, my body refused to respond to the ventilator as expected and the ARDS worsened. They were puzzled and concerned at the bleak outlook. It was a new disease and there were no libraries of data to access as with other better-known diseases. To make matters worse, I was not the only case of COVID-19 they were dealing with who was not responding as expected and new cases were coming into hospital daily. Families were losing loved ones from this new disease at an alarming rate. Would there be enough beds, staff and equipment or would the system be tested to beyond the limits?

Amanda read furiously, as she does, and discussed the possibility of various drugs to try to help my condition. Remdesevir, an antiviral drug, had been suggested as a treatment for severe COVID-19 but was still being tested in medical research and there was no proof that it would help. Over successive days, the initial positivity disappeared and there was no good news towards the end of the first week in ICU. The doctors phoned Amanda back to counsel her that the situation was looking bleak. Our family rallied round her. My brothers were a tower of strength and would speak to Amanda several times each day. At this point, she was self-isolating having been in close contact with me and did not know if she or indeed one of our children might become as unwell as me. It must have been a dreadful time for all of them. My oldest brother, John, has been a doctor for 30 years and would also keep in touch with the hospital to provide Amanda with the most accurate information. He did this whilst carrying out his own job selflessly.

As the week unfolded, it was clear that further treatment would be needed as nothing was working and I was dying. Amanda had resigned herself to the fact that when the phone rang it was not going to be good news and she thought that, eventually, the hospital would phone to tell her that I had died. There was nothing that she could do and indeed nothing that medicine could do. It must have been horrendous for her and the family, particularly as she was not able to visit. News bulletins were filled with bad news about COVID-19 and the numbers of lives it was claiming, including those of the relatively young. This must also have been horrific for the medical team who were doing everything they could in very challenging circumstances.

I continued to deteriorate and a few days later the situation was described as 'precarious'. I suffered a collapsed lung (pneumothorax) and this was being monitored closely as this can be very serious. At one point on being turned from prone to supine, this became an emergency life or death situation and a chest drain had to be inserted as an urgent procedure. The doctors were very worried, although fortunately, I stabilised and was proned again. The doctors contacted colleagues in Aberdeen at the Scottish national ECMO (extracorporeal membrane oxygenation) unit to discuss my case and as the stable situation could be maintained, the decision was made to keep me on the existing treatment regime in Dundee. The next day, there was further discussion with the ECMO team and as gas exchange on the ventilator was stable, I was to be kept in Dundee but I needed to be turned supine to alleviate the pressure on the front of my body. Having done this, oxygenation worsened and I had to be proned quickly. The medical team in Dundee had reached the limit of what they could do to keep me alive.

Artificially oxygenating my blood and removing carbon dioxide using ECMO life support was the only option left to keep me alive. ECMO is a last-gasp treatment for acute heart or lung failure that has potential to be reversed, but only where it is not responding to 'conventional' treatment. ECMO cannot be used where the underlying condition is not compatible with normal life, the patient is elderly or has poor quality of life due to, for example, a tumour, obesity, or where there is a substantial risk of systemic bleeding due to blood thinning drugs (anticoagulation) necessary for the blood to flow round the ECMO machine and associated tubing. Patients who have been kept alive by conventional therapy for too long or where they have a fatal diagnosis are not suitable for ECMO. Although I was in multi-organ failure, I was regarded as a relatively young patient who with the support of ECMO might be able to survive. I now know as I write that of the six patients in Scotland who were referred for ECMO during the first wave of COVID-19, only two of us survived. Amanda and the family were ecstatic that I might be given the chance to live. They were keen that no time was wasted and that I was put onto ECMO as soon as possible.

The problem was there were three other patients being referred to the Aberdeen ECMO team at the same time and the team could only travel for one patient at a time. They had to prioritise the sickest and most precarious, which was me. I am told they spent most of that day travelling all over Scotland collecting patients. The Dundee team needed to prepare me for the ECMO treatment, they needed to book an operating theatre, a radiographer and a plan to get me to the operating theatre safely and have a blood transfusion ready, but the sands of time were not on anyone's side, they were running out and this was all before I was to be transferred to Aberdeen to continue the ECMO treatment, still some 70 miles away.

The Aberdeen ECMO retrieval team travelled to Dundee and along with one of the Dundee ICU consultants, took me to the operating theatre to install a line in each femoral vein in my groin and a line in my right internal jugular vein passing to the right atrium of my heart for so-called VVV (triple venous) circuit ECMO. To do this, I needed to be lying on my back for access to my groin and neck. My oxygen saturation level dropped to the 60% level and considerable blood pressure support was needed. The lines were inserted fairly quickly but getting them secured and packaging me up on the transfer trolley and ensuring I was stable enough to be moved took over two hours. The team were amazed to see the colour of my skin improve as the ECMO machine took over and my blood oxygen level reached 95%, the highest it had been for some days. The amount of blood pressure support could then also be reduced and I was finally stable as oxygen was moving round my body. It was a stressful time for everyone involved, particularly as I was now edging ever closer to death.

I was urgently transferred to Aberdeen with an ECMO transport team consisting of two consultants and two ECMO specialist nurses to ensure the blood circulating in the machine and re-entering my body contained the appropriate levels of blood gases. It must have been a quick journey by ambulance but a very stressful trip for the ECMO team with such a sick patient to look after in such a confined space. As I had discovered when becoming ill, ambulances are not as comfortable a ride as I would have thought. I am generally on time for most events and if anything like to arrive early. Indeed, I was born on the due date my mother was given and attribute being on time to my start in life. The question in everyone's mind at this point was would I make it in time. Any thoughts of timekeeping now were irrelevant, it was all about survival and I was gravely ill.

The ECMO machine works as a bypass machine by pumping the blood round the circuit and the oxygenator and exchanges oxygen and carbon dioxide in the blood. The blood coming out of the body is dark due to the relatively high carbon dioxide levels and low oxygen levels but is much brighter in colour on return.

Anticoagulation drugs are needed to prevent clotting and this needs to be monitored regularly. As well as this, the regular vital parameters such as cardiac functioning and arterial blood gases are monitored frequently to determine when ECMO can be stopped. Amanda was warned that there are a number of significant complications that can result from ECMO: a brain haemorrhage, direct brain damage and brain death, unexplained coma, fatal sepsis, blood clots resulting in lung or heart damage, blood vessel damage and heparin-induced thrombocytopaenia (a potentially devastating immune mediated adverse drug reaction caused by the emergence of antibodies that activate platelets in the presence of heparin, resulting in a drop in the number of platelets, risking bleeding to death). All very worrying.

In the end, the ambulance made good time and I was transferred to the ECMO unit, a small area in the ICU ward. I was hooked up to the various machines and ECMO was continued in earnest. Amanda and the family were given the devastating news that ECMO required a significant amount of resilience from my body to be able to survive the treatment and it was no panacea. Even in the best situations, an ECMO patient has only a 60% chance of survival. Amanda was prepared yet again for a dreadful outcome and was told that I might not survive. A new CT scan revealed that my lungs had been severely damaged by the COVID-19 pneumonia and that they were only operating at 5% capacity. The irony was, that by this point I was COVID-19 negative but the disease and my immune response had resulted in so much damage.

It was not possible for Amanda or any other family to visit me in Aberdeen as the lockdown restrictions banned all hospital visiting. Instead, my family all participated in the 'Clap for Carers'. As I was no longer a patient in Dundee, the bag with my belongings was picked up and taken home. Amanda noticed as she unpacked the bag that it contained my glasses and worried how I would cope without them. She therefore asked the ECMO team the next day if she could bring them to Aberdeen and duly made the journey along with Anna later that week. She had no expectation of being able to see me and indeed the security guard on duty at the main hospital entrance would not let anyone past. Having telephoned the ECMO unit to let them know that they had arrived, one of the wonderful ECMO nurses came down to collect my glasses and provided an update. Whilst there was no good news yet again, the nurse had realised that Amanda and Anna had made a long journey and brought them some sandwiches, biscuits and a drink. They were delighted at the kindness of the nurse and knew that I was in very caring hands. They drove home wondering how I was getting on but knew with each communication that the situation was worsening by the day.

Amanda was naturally preparing for the worst. She had been advised by the close family that she would need considerable support if I did not survive and there was worry about how our adult children would deal with the situation if I died. Jonathan was at home at this point and provided considerable practical and emotional support to Amanda. Anna was at home as well and can read her mother's emotions well and provide the necessary assistance. She, like so many other people had been sent home from work on the government furlough scheme so would receive 80% of her salary and would return to work once the lockdown was lifted. Colin, our youngest, did what he always does and worked as hard as possible. He threw himself into work and did various additional shifts to cover for colleagues who were sick, isolating or caring for others. He was told that he was the hardest working employee in the company. The major concern was for Alexander who lived on his own. He had been reluctant to come back to the family home at the start of the pandemic as he did not want to mix with either Amanda or me in case we had inadvertently brought the virus home from work. How true his premonition turned out to be. Amanda needed to have her adult children on hand as disaster after disaster occurred and therefore Anna and her partner, Lawrence, were asked to collect him. They had the difficult situation of confronting him with the potentially tragic news and to bring him home with the possessions he would need for the next few weeks.

My medical situation did not improve on the ECMO machine. Meanwhile, day after day, Amanda worked from home as a deputy head teacher, a role that had a wide range of responsibilities, most notably running a school in conjunction with the head teacher and the staff. At this point in lockdown, schools were closed and parents were expected to help with educating their children at home whilst teachers would provide digital educational material as needed. It was a challenging time for everyone. Amanda did as she always does and carried out her job to the best of her abilities and beyond. I am sure this helped take her mind off my struggle with life during the day and would have helped with a degree of 'normality' even though the world was far from normal. Amanda would speak at length with the ECMO doctors and nurses each morning and evening. There was rarely any good news and they had prepared her for the worst news possible on many occasions. Amanda, however, had enormous faith in me and kept saying to the staff that they didn't know me as well as she did and that I would fight this horrible disease. Amanda kept willing me on and encouraged me from afar. I knew that we had a very strong marriage, but I didn't ever want to test our bond in such a way. Amanda's best friend, Julia, would phone daily and would come round to see Amanda to comfort her when she could. They had a very strong friendship and knew how to support each other on every occasion. What was to happen next was to test my body and Amanda's faith in my survival to the limit.

CHAPTER 5

In the Arms of Morpheus

MY BODY was struggling to stay alive with COVID-19 and the cytokine storm was causing chaos in every organ, every system and every tissue. The combination of the ventilator and the ECMO treatment was arduous on my body as well and maintaining an adequate level of oxygenation was proving to be a challenge for the medical team. Alarmingly, my oxygen saturation levels frequently dropped to around 40%. The normal level is above 95%. It must have been an extremely worrying time for the medical and nursing staff who couldn't work out why this was happening. They decided to do a bronchoscopy using a fibre-optic camera to examine my airways. It did not provide any additional reason why my lungs were not performing well even on ECMO but at least it confirmed there were no other problems (co-morbidity) affecting my condition. The medical staff protected Amanda from the numerical detail of my blood oxygen levels to help her keep as strong as possible. How she managed to keep composed I do not know. She later told me that she was given two weeks of compassionate leave by her boss in the education department as the situation was so bleak. After this she returned to work, trying to balance her emotions with the needs of the children, teachers and other staff at school. What a remarkable wife. This is one aspect of Amanda that never fails to surprise me.

Unfortunately, the only way the ECMO team could keep my blood oxygen levels up was to supplement the ECMO system with fresh blood transfusions and I was given a total of 56 units of blood and various blood products to keep me alive. At least I had donated blood on 46 occasions prior to becoming sick so in retrospect whilst I feel guilty that I used vital stocks of blood and blood products while on ECMO, I have at least made a contribution over the 20 plus years that I have been donating. The NHS Blood Transplant service astounds me. It is there when anyone needs it, yet there is no fanfare for the staff and patients who provide the expertise or indeed the blood and organs for the system to function. Even though it is part of the NHS, it seems to operate in a slightly autonomous and very efficient way. The service has evolved significantly over the years to be a beacon of excellence in patient care during donation sessions and in the compassion shown to the families of organ donors at precisely the worst point in time. I had made it known to my family on many occasions that I would have no objection to any of my organs being made available for transplant in the event of my death. Had I died at this point, I guess none of my organs would have been in any fit state to be of use to anyone else. My body was suffering the ravages of not only COVID-19 but also the cytokine storm and it was in poor condition. Even the doctors did not know what was to come.

COVID-19 and the cytokine storm had now attacked every corner of my body and the multi-organ failure situation was not improving. I was more dead than alive. As a result I also suffered a number of other medical crises. On two occasions, I suffered blood clots in my legs which broke off and travelled round my veins to cause pulmonary embolisms. These can be life threatening and a good friend, Drew, has suffered a pulmonary embolism on two occasions. He believed he was dying both times. Luckily, the medical team treated these early for me with clot-busting drugs to prevent my life being endangered any further. Looking back, this was not surprising as COVID-19 has such an effect on the vascular system in the body. Indeed, it is primarily a disease that attacks small blood vessels by causing micro-clots, which can snowball into much larger clots. These cause the significant damage in patients who suffer the critical illness form of COVID-19 along with the cytokine storm. Routine treatment was not effective as I became allergic to the standard drug, heparin, used to thin the blood and prevent further clots. I was now suffering from heparin-induced thrombocytopaenia and could have bled to death without swift action. A substitute was therefore required, Argatroban, and this has ongoing implications for me for the rest of my life.

I was also unlucky to suffer a second pneumothorax, a collapsed lung which again was not surprising due to the severe pneumonia that I had experienced. Amanda later told me that another chest drain was used to help re-inflate it without any further surgical intervention. This must have been inserted very carefully as I have not been able to identify a second scar in my armpit for the tube from the 'fish tank' that is used to provide negative pressure to re-inflate the lung. It is known as a 'fish tank' as the drain tank has various chambers but bubbles as the patient coughs, in a similar manner to the tropical tank we have at home. This pneumothorax, presumably, was equally worrying for the ECMO medical staff who were well aware of the implications of trying to artificially ventilate a collapsed lung of a patient on active ECMO who had been lifeless due to oxygen deprivation. Equally concerningly, I continued to show signs of sepsis. My immune system had managed to clear the COVID-19 infection but was presumably exhausted having become overwhelmed. The immune system fascinates me. How the body manages to deal with bacterial, fungal and viral invaders is simply incredible. The immune system primarily has two main functions, cell-mediated and humoral immunity. The key difference between the two is that the humoral system works using antibodies produced by B lymphocytes and is so named as these are produced in the humours, or body fluids. Cell-mediated immunity, on the other hand, involves the activation of phagocytes, T-lymphocytes and the release of various cytokines in response to an invader. Put simply, the humoral part of the immune system primarily acts on viruses that infect us, whilst the cell-mediated part is triggered by bacterial and fungal invaders. There is a degree of overlap, which I find reassuring and whilst the humoral system had now killed all of the COVID-19 virus particles, my body and indeed my humours were weak. It was no laughing matter.

My weakened immune system allowed the pseudomonas bacteria to start colonising my respiratory system, which no longer extended from my nose and mouth to the alveolar sacs deep inside my lungs, but now involved the ventilator tubing entering my mouth and the ventilator itself. Clearly my immune system could not send blood containing all the important cell-mediated and humoral immune components round the plastic tubing of the ventilator system and could therefore only deal with any bugs that physically entered my body. Hospitals by their very nature are warm places with ill patients and naturally there are plenty of opportunities for infections. Pseudomonas is rife in respiratory patients with a depressed immune system.

Pseudomonas sepsis can be life threatening and I required urgent treatment to prevent the immune system causing yet another cytokine storm and causing more self-inflicted damage. Aggressive treatment was started to avoid any serious consequences and potential death. Treatment was complicated as the first antibiotics used had no effect and the pseudomonas count in my blood continued to rise exponentially. It became apparent that I was now allergic to one of the end-stage antibiotics, vancomycin. I had no idea before coming into hospital that I was allergic to either heparin or vancomycin but was aware that as I got older, I had been picking up allergies. I started beekeeping a few years ago and on two occasions, I have suffered a severe allergic response, angioedema, when experiencing multiple stings which interestingly manifests as an airway restriction, hives and a rather dramatic facial and neck rash. I didn't have the opportunity to forewarn the medical staff that I was aware of an increasing number of allergies and the likelihood of a cytokine storm. It is interesting to note that as I write, the term 'cytokine storm' has now become well known not only in medical circles, but also amongst the general public.

I remained unresponsive whilst on the ECMO treatment and there were many stormy days and nights. Even though I was in an induced coma, I was not reacting to the normal stimuli, including pain from squeezing an earlobe. The Glasgow Coma Scale (GCS) is used throughout the world to assess the responsiveness of patients and I had been trained in its use in the early part of my career when working in Glasgow in the facial trauma service. It provides a metric to determine the level of consciousness and the likelihood of, ultimately, survival. It measures eye opening response, best verbal response and spontaneous motor response of e.g. fingers and toes. Although I was in an induced coma, the doctors would reduce the sedation periodically to assess my responsiveness. I initially had the lowest score for each domain which is given a score of one point for each, totalling three. This is the lowest score possible. It would not have given anyone confidence that I would survive this ordeal with a score of three, particularly since this was a long way from the normal score of 15 for a compos mentis adult. One day, my left eye had a dilated pupil and the right eye was normal. A dilated pupil is known as a 'blown pupil' and is of concern as it can be a symptom of a brain injury from either physical trauma or a stroke.

Clearly I had not suffered any trauma so a brain CT scan was taken to assess if there had been any brain damage resulting from any blood flow changes due to the anticoagulant potentially causing a stroke. There are only four arteries that supply blood to the brain, the right and left internal and external carotid arteries. The internal carotid arteries by nature are deep within the neck and supply the base of the brain, whilst the external carotid arteries are close to the surface of the skin of the neck and feed the face and then the outer surface of the brain. There is limited scope for any crossover between the subdivisions of the internal and external carotid arteries within the brain and any blockage usually results in a stroke. In retrospect, a stroke would not have been unexpected if COVID-19 had caused micro-clots or even substantial clots within the blood vessels in and around my brain. It was not surprising when a small brain haemorrhage was detected by the CT scan. Amanda was told by the doctors that this could result in brain damage, but it would be difficult to test as I was in an induced coma. What would this mean? Would it be serious? The medical staff did their best to allay Amanda's fears and at the end of the day, they were trying to save my life; a small brain haemorrhage might not be the end of the world. Callum and Douglas had gone over to Mum's to celebrate her birthday, but it was hardly the day anyone wanted.

The final medical disaster was to my kidneys and this had occurred early on in ICU. Kidney disease is either acute or chronic and whilst COVID-19 could have damaged the intricate blood vessel architecture of my kidneys directly, the micro-clotting issue could have caused long-term infarctions (blockages leading to tissue death) as well, which would be both chronic and permanent. Furthermore, the antibiotics and vasopressor medications I was now on for sepsis and low blood pressure could also cause acute kidney injury. Kidney failure in an ICU patient usually marks a poor indicator for survival with less than 50% of those with kidney failure eventually surviving. Frequent blood tests were done to assess the situation. One of the key molecules measured to assess kidney health is creatinine, a waste product from the breakdown of metabolised muscle tissue. The normal amount of creatinine in the blood for a man is around 1 milligram per decilitre. My levels at this point were increasing on a logarithmic scale and at one point, the level reached 600, which meant that I was suffering acute kidney failure and that there was significant muscle metabolism taking place. My body was in a terrible state. I was destroying muscle tissue and was in kidney failure. Not only do the kidneys expel water as part of urine, they also get rid of excess electrolytes such as potassium, magnesium and calcium along with urea and creatinine. The kidneys also expel various acidic products that are too toxic for the lungs to deal with. With this combination of respiratory and kidney failure, I was in danger of going into uncontrolled acidosis and edging further towards death. Kidney dialysis was started in Dundee and continued in Aberdeen resulting in more tubes being inserted into my body with further risks for infection, bleeding and so on. In Aberdeen, the catheter was inserted into the subclavian vein just below the collar bone and advanced towards the chest and another chest X-ray to confirm the position of the cannula. Although the dialysis used in Dundee had been intermittent, dialysis for acute kidney injuries whilst on ECMO runs continuously. As a new disease, the long-term effects of COVID-19 on the kidneys were unknown and could be serious. Amanda was informed that dialysis might be needed in the longer-term and this was information that needed time to come to terms with. Moreover, two new phenomena were occurring in COVID-19 patients requiring dialysis. Only 10% of ICU patients normally require dialysis but due to the cytokine storm, many more patients now required dialysis and hospitals were in danger of running out of dialysis machines rather than ventilators as publicised by the media earlier in the first wave of COVID-19. Moreover, the micro-clotting issue was causing chaos with the filters in dialysis machines which were either aborting the dialysing cycle or sounding the alarm system requiring much more frequent filter changes. Some hospitals were at risk of running out of filters.

The doctors phoned Callum urgently. They were concerned that Amanda was not able to digest how critical my condition was. A new CT showed that my lungs had deteriorated again and whilst other patients had improved quicker, I was going the wrong way. There was also an infection around one of the ECMO lines and it was not possible to replace the infected tube. Everything hinged on the antibiotics addressing this next crisis. The doctors were

'DYING TO LIVE'

also concerned about the effect of COVID-19 on my liver as my liver function tests were not normal on many occasions. Furthermore, they monitored my heart closely in case COVID-19 and the cytokine storm had caused damage to this vital organ. Although my heart remained strong, the complications caused by COVID-19 were serious. These complications were very concerning to the medical team and Amanda, not to mention my family and friends. Amanda and my brothers were naturally concerned that even if I were to survive, what quality of life would I have if any of the medical complications caused permanent disease or disability.

Nobody knew if I would survive yet my extended family, friends and colleagues wanted updates on my condition. I am usually quite good at communicating by email, text and using social media. I use the phone a lot at work but am less inclined to phone people for a chat as everyone is so busy these days. The one person I do phone regularly is my mum. I also phone Amanda when work takes me away overnight, and this gives us an opportunity to find out what the other has been doing that day. Family, friends and colleagues were concerned that I had dropped out of all communication rapidly and as this was unusual, everyone was worried.

My family were tremendous and worked out a communication system to cascade information about my condition. Whilst my friends did not want to intrude, they kept in touch with my brothers and also set up a communication chain to provide updates to everyone. I have many good friends that are also colleagues and they managed to keep those close to me at work in the loop. This amazing group of friends decided to have an information blackout across our building as they had no idea if I would survive, and they did not want to intrude on what was the hardest time for any family to go through. The level of support for Amanda from other sources was exceptional. Her phone would buzz with messages from her friends and family keeping her going. My brothers and her parents would call her daily, and at times several times each day to check in on her own health as well as having an update on my condition. The postman would bring more mail than usual every day. Amanda and the family opened cards from people in my professional life that they had never met; flowers and hampers were delivered from family and friends, from the British Orthodontic Society, the Royal College of Surgeons of Edinburgh and the Consultant Orthodontists Group. My closest friends at work also sent Amanda a huge floral display. I just wish I had been at home to see many of the lovely flowers that arrived!

I later discovered just how much support was pushing me and the family on. The ability to communicate instantly across the globe worked in my favour as my many family members, colleagues and friends live in various parts of the world. Coupled with this, my brothers, friends and colleagues also connected with their families, friends and colleagues resulting in a huge network of people keeping our family in their thoughts and praying for us. Friends and family friends composed and recorded songs, recorded messages and sent these to be played for me by whatever means. My cousin's husband played 'Highland Cathedral' on his church organ for me, my friends at work wrote a special tune just for me with very personal lyrics, even conscripting a spare husband to play the guitar in the background and one of Callum's friends in Perth, Australia, performed a rendition of the Hollies version of 'He Ain't Heavy, He's My Brother' specially for me. If only these could be played in a book, I would share these with the reader.

My best friends were selfless with their messages, ensuring they were providing me with an update on their lives, sport, politics, current affairs and their own personal commentary on life. All seven continents were covered – Wow! I later discovered that there were multiple prayer groups in the UK, USA, India, Australia, New Zealand and in other countries that were praying specifically for me and my family. I have found this incredibly humbling but am nevertheless delighted that people took time to think of and pray for me. One of our friends had written a special piece of music for our wedding and played piano at the ceremony. Amanda asked him to record it to see if this would help encourage me. I am sure it did as it has a special place in our hearts, and it will have resonated in my subconscious. Amanda would also spray my aftershave on my pillow so that she did not forget what I smelled like. Amanda is an agnostic, but this was the time when she felt closest to a superior power and asked on many occasions for me to be spared with the following prayer:

This prayer is for my beloved husband Grant. Grant is strong and is overcoming the burdens on his body. The healing intelligence that created his body is now banishing these burdens allowing his lungs to fill with air and his kidneys to return to their normal function. All problems are removed and the wholeness and beauty of the life principle are manifest in every atom of his being. Grant is open and receptive to the healing currents which are flowing like a river, restoring him to perfect health, harmony and wellbeing. All difficulties are washed away by the infinite ocean of love flowing through him and it is so. I know and decree that health, harmony and wellbeing are now being expressed in Grant's mind and body.

With so many close calls with the Grim Reaper, evidently it was not my time to die.

CHAPTER 6

Still Sleeping

MY CLINICAL WORK sees me on a daily basis working with evidence-based healthcare. Consequently, I would have wanted the doctors and medical teams treating me to follow best practice and use evidence-based guidelines. I appreciate that I am very mainstream in my clinical work, after all, I work for the NHS and one of the responsibilities of a consultant is to ensure that the patients that are being treated by me or my team, are provided with care that has been tested as being effective and efficient. New and untested treatments are not used, except in research where it is overseen by the research governance team in our health board and university. They are fully independent and provide ethical approval, intellectual sponsorship and regular reporting of each research study to ensure research participants are well cared for and any unexpected findings or unintended harms are addressed. Our research laboratory is fortunate that it has not had to discontinue a trial due to unplanned events, a situation I know many colleagues have been in.

The difficulty with my period of sickness was that COVID-19 was a new disease with little evidence relating to prevention and treatment. After all, by the time I was critically unwell and in a coma, the disease had only been known about for four months. Since I don't take any risks with my patients, normally I would not want anyone to take a chance with a new, untried or untested drug treatment on me, unless it was part of a research study. I was now, however, in dire straits and I would have sanctioned anything as a research participant. Indeed, I would have wanted Amanda and the rest of the family to encourage the doctors to enter me into a COVID research programme as it is a well-known fact that patients in research studies have better outcomes, even those in untreated control groups.

I would not sanction the use of alternative treatments and whimsical ideas on my patients so would not want these used on me at this point of life or death in my journey. That is not to say that I am critical of the benefits of complementary therapies. Homeopathy, aromatherapy, acupuncture, osteopathy, chiropractor treatments and herbal medicine do not help in orthodontics, but may reduce treatment side effects. In fact, my team has carried out a randomised controlled trial of acupressure to find out if it reduces the discomfort of fixed braces and interestingly, we found that acupressure was as effective as paracetamol. However, this was not the time for complementary therapies.

Although there were many doctors in the ECMO team, including one poignantly named Dr Casino, at no point did they take any unnecessary gambles. This is in fact exactly what I would have done as the motto for Clan McIntyre is *per ardua* which means 'through difficulty'. The clan motto is important to me in my daily work. My belief is that most challenges are achievable, they just need perseverance through the hard days as a mix of 99% perspiration and 1% inspiration usually works. One of my former research students even bought me a mug with this printed on the side! I am not afraid of hard work and constantly tell those around me that hard work never causes anyone harm. I am sure the *per ardua* spirit helped those caring for me by encouraging me to keep going.

I have no memory of my time undergoing ECMO treatment even though Amanda spoke to me daily by video call. Each call must have been very difficult as it was a one-sided conversation and there is a limit to how much even Amanda could have found to talk about each day. Nonetheless, Amanda made sure that during each call she would tell me how much she loved me and would try to convince my ailing body and wandered mind that I could not only fight the situation, but that I would beat it. She would encourage me to speak back to her, even though I could not due to the breathing tube attached to the ventilator. Trying to encourage me to form words in my head was the first step on the road to speaking. She would also ask me to look at her and wave even though I was totally lifeless. It must have been dreadfully difficult to keep composed during these calls and whilst I am sure the nursing staff are used to relatives providing encouragement for the patient, I doubt they will have come across someone as determined as Amanda! Sometimes she would speak to me for an hour.

Amanda continued to speak twice daily to the nursing and medical staff. Some days, she would receive lots of information, particularly if it had been a good day, but on other days, there would be little to report or indeed the nursing and medical staff would be careful with the information they would share with her, particularly if the news was negative. Amanda eventually reasoned with herself that no progress was a positive as it meant my recovery was not going backwards. Sadly, 'no news' was the case on many days, and it is testament to Amanda's strength that she coped so well during this period. On other occasions, video calls would have to be curtailed as an emerging problem was identified that needed urgent attention. Naturally, the nursing staff were compassionate and told Amanda that I was tired or needed some treatment.

The level of interest in experimental antiviral drugs peaked when the US regulators allowed the use of Remdesivir, with early studies showing COVID-19 recovery time could be cut by 31%. Amanda seized on this as an opportunity to improve the potential outcome for me. She asked the consultants to consider a compassionate trial of Remdesivir, but they told her that it was unlikely to be of any use as I was clear of COVID-19. There were no virus particles left in my body now so the drug would have no virus to kill.

This was not the first experience of ICU for Amanda. She had spent many weeks with Alexander (her third child) in paediatric ICU when he was a baby as he had contracted respiratory syncytial virus and was extremely unwell. This was a hugely troubling period for her - to see her child's life hanging by a thread must have been a very difficult experience. Despite having another close relative gravely ill in ICU, Amanda coped amazingly well. She told them that I would take any challenge head on and encouraged them to keep me alive at all costs.

On one occasion I was deteriorating again and, having spoken to the nursing team at length, Amanda was advised that there was little hope left. Although she was advised that care was not being withdrawn at any point, she was told that if there were no signs of positivity there would need to be discussion with all of the family. I later discovered that a young woman who was admitted on the same night as me and also went for ECMO treatment died suddenly. I cannot begin to think how horrendous this must have been for her family.

Amanda was aware of speculation about various other drug treatments for COVID-19. In fact, this was never far from the news. One of these was the anti-malarial drug hydroxychloroquine (HCQ), which is also used to treat symptoms of the debilitating immune-mediated conditions rheumatoid arthritis and discoid or systemic lupus erythematosus. It was one of the most controversial therapies proposed for COVID-19. Donald Trump championed the use of chloroquine and HCQ for COVID-19. Trump's comments led to a shortage of both drugs in the US and panic buying in Africa and South Asia.

Trump later stated publicly that he had been taking hydroxy-chloroquine with zinc and an initial dose of azithromycin. The

WHO and partners set up the Solidarity clinical trial to investigate COVID-19 treatments in hospital comparing Remdesevir,
Lopinavir/Ritonavir, Lopinavir/Ritonavir combined with
interferon-beta and hydroxychloroquine or chloroquine. It was
one of the quickest organised multinational trials ever. Nearly
5,000 patients in 21 countries were recruited in three months
and in total, 12,000 patients were recruited spanning 30 countries.

The WHO suspended and then terminated the hydroxychloroquine
arm of the trial as it provided no benefit to hospitalised, severely
infected COVID-19 patients. In addition to hydroxychloroquine
having little benefit, the Lopinavir and interferon regimens also
appeared to have little or no effect on hospitalised COVID-19
patients. In short, hydroxychloroquine is a dangerous drug to
administer. When used with a patient also taking the antibiotic
azithromycin, research has shown it can cause a 65% increase in
cardiac mortality. Even on its own, hydroxychloroquine can in
the short term cause blurred vision, focusing difficulties,
distorted vision, blind spots, trouble reading, changes in colour
vision and increased sensitivity to light, and eventually
irreversible retinal damage. Trump can be held responsible for
this piece of 'fake news'. I was clear of COVID-19 by this point, so
HCQ and chloroquine would not have been of any benefit.

Amanda wondered if there was any other drug that could help and
regularly asked the ECMO team. Steroids are an anti-inflammatory
medication and the logic behind it is that by dampening down
inflammation and the cytokine storm, survival might be possible.
The RECOVERY Trial sponsored by the NHS had been set up
to test dexamethasone for COVID-19 patients on mechanical
ventilators and those who required supplemental oxygen. A total
of 6,425 participants were recruited. I was not entered as I was
critically ill being septic and in multi-organ failure.

The medical team discussed my case at a national ECMO
conference with experts deliberating on the progress of each

patient and also making suggestions on what else could be done. One of my consultants spoke to Callum after the meeting to let him know that they were at the end of the road. Other less ill patients were dying and trying steroids in line with the RECOVERY trial would be *'the last roll of the dice'*. It was now a gamble, all or nothing. This was described to Amanda as being 'a very risky strategy' since my body was still fighting the effects of being septic as well as being in multi-organ failure. If this did not work, they had no further options and although death was not talked about openly, Amanda knew exactly what was at stake. She had never been so worried about me. This was it, and had I been a cat, all but one of the nine lives were now gone.

The doctors gave me five days of high dose methylprednisolone and waited. Everyone waited. Everyone in the family was not only clapping for the carers but also willing me on through this most difficult period. Somehow, I began to stabilise. Updates started to mention 'no change' and 'settled overnight' which was an improvement from previous harrowing reports. The doctors reported a small improvement after a chest CT scan, which everyone appreciated was actually a huge move in the right direction. Finally.

As the weeks rolled on, there were signs of improvement in my lungs. The decision was taken to try reducing the level of sedation to see how I would respond. With initial attempts, things did not go as expected and I was rapidly re-sedated. On day 39, there were the first signs of positivity from the high dose steroids. They were starting to have an effect and the gamble was paying off. My eyelids flickered and on command from the nurses, I was able to move a finger. My GCS score had increased from 3 to 10 out of 15. The medical and nursing team were delighted with this. Amanda was, not surprisingly, overjoyed and wanted me to repeat this for her on multiple occasions. It must have been such a relief that there were signs of life returning and her thoughts turned from despair to hope.

Callum had kept in touch with the ECMO nurses and had provided them with lots of information about my life as well as photos from various moments in my life. They put the photos on the wall next to my bed and they would point to them to tell me who was in each picture. The nurses would chat to me as if I were fully conscious. I think this is an excellent way of keeping a patient connected with their family and friends while comatose. Callum let the nursing staff know that my son, Colin's 21st birthday was coming soon and that I would not want to miss the occasion. The nursing staff were excellent and organised a birthday card from me and because I could not write, they managed to put my fingerprints on the card instead. On his birthday, the nurses gave me the option of video calling Colin from the bed or the adjacent chair. Apparently, I was insistent that I should sit in the chair. It must have been a terrible upheaval to have to hoist me and move all the various pieces of equipment and I now appreciate how much effort the staff put in. Colin duly video called and although I could not speak, the nurses helped me communicate by lifting my finger as needed. I have no memory of this, but it must have been disconcerting for Colin to see his father in the ECMO unit looking so unwell. I was, however, alive and making tiny steps of progress.

As the days moved on and I made slight improvements, there was hope that I might not only survive the disease that had nearly claimed my life but also survive all the complications. The nurses were tremendous and looked after all aspects of my personal care. I didn't know it at the time, but they spoke to me continually while working around me and were so cheerful in everything they did. They gave me a daily bedbath and pampered me like a baby. Nothing was too much trouble for them; they looked after every aspect of my little world. The nurses knew my job as an orthodontist was important to me and Amanda had explained to them that I had a degree of fixation with my own dental health. The nurses were not able to floss my teeth, but they took good care to brush my teeth as best they could each day. Apparently as

'DYING TO LIVE'

the sedation was reduced and my condition improved, I used my fingers to give the nurses a score out of ten for brushing my teeth!

Somehow, eventually everyone's prayers, positive energy and hopes were answered. I had defied the low odds of survival, although I was still more dead than alive. On day 42, the decision was taken to disconnect the oxygenator within the ECMO machine and the circulating pump was left connected for a further 8 days. In total, I was on the ECMO life support machine for 50 days. At this point, it was fully withdrawn as I was responding to the ventilator spontaneously and was maintaining good levels of blood oxygenation. The focus suddenly shifted from mere survival and for the first time, rehabilitation was mentioned to Amanda. It must have been a massive relief for the medical and nursing teams who had worked so hard to revive me and to get me to that point. It must have been an amazing piece of news to share with family and friends. I had had the longest ECMO run of all the COVID-19 patients treated during the first wave in Scotland.

The journey was far from over and I was extremely weak and nobody knew if any of the damage to my liver, kidneys, heart, brain or gut would be temporary or permanent. I was later told that a protracted period of ECMO is unusual and is often associated with brain damage. This must have been concerning and nobody would have wanted me to survive but end up with a poor quality of life.

Until this stage, the ventilator had been inserted via my mouth into my lungs using an endotracheal tube. It was decided as I improved that changing this to a tracheostomy would help in making me more comfortable and therefore allow the medical team to wean me off the ventilator at the point I became more independent, if I could make it past the acute illness phase. In addition, the tracheostomy would require less effort to oxygenate my blood. I was taken back to the operating theatre again.

As I write, I acknowledge the fact that I am grateful to my career for preparing me for the hospitalisation, ICU and operating theatre episodes, having spent nearly 30 years working in the NHS. Although no two operating theatres are identical, they all contain the same equipment and are broadly similar. This environment would not have unsettled me and although I have no recollection, I am sure I would have felt relatively comfortable knowing what was going to happen during the procedure. I had after all, requested to be put on a ventilator so many weeks previously and had asked the medical team to save my life. I had known at that point that I would have sanctioned anything that would have improved my chances of survival. The tracheostomy was duly inserted through a small incision made in my neck below the vocal cords.

I remember working in hospitals in my early career and being part of the team in the operating theatre when a tracheostomy was required either as a planned procedure or in an emergency situation. Emergency tracheostomies are rather scary to watch as by nature they are life-saving procedures and speed rather than finesse is required. A planned tracheostomy on the other hand can be performed more carefully with regard to the final scar and avoidance of local nerves and blood vessels. Once the skin has been perforated, the trachea (windpipe) is accessed below the vocal cords and cut before the tracheostomy tube is inserted, the cuff blown up and secured, a skin dressing is applied to soak up secretions and a band secured around the patient's neck to hold it in place. Finally, the cuff at the base of the tracheostomy tube, deep inside the trachea is inflated to seal the trachea from the mouth and the lungs. It then becomes the only portal into the lungs. And if needed, as in my case, a ventilator can be reattached.

Having been returned to the ECMO unit, my condition slowly improved over the following days and it was decided that I was well enough to go back to Ninewells Hospital. I am sure this must have been a great moment for the ECMO team having had to rush to Ninewells so many weeks previously to retrieve me and rush me to their unit in Aberdeen. Whilst I was by no means healthy at this point, I was in a much better condition and I am sure the transfer was less stressful for everyone involved, and a great deal safer for the patient! I have no memory of the initial Ninewells HDU/ICU time or the ECMO period, although curiously I have a memory of the transfer from Aberdeen back to Dundee. I felt the trolley going in the ambulance. I recall being 'clunked' into place and the paramedic, ICU doctor and nursing team ensuring I was fully strapped in for the journey. I also recall having to be cleaned at some point during the journey as some excreta had escaped from the flexi-pipe in my bottom. Whilst my memory of this is rather unpleasant, I understood what was needed to be done at the time and appreciate that trying to clean a sedated patient in an ambulance moving at high speed must have been quite a challenge. To me, the journey seemed to take forever.

I was repatriated into ICU in Ninewells Hospital. I think the use of 'repatriated' when patients return to their original hospital is a delightful choice of word. It suggests there is a degree of loyalty of patients towards their 'home' hospital. This is very much the case for me since I have spent so much time over the years in Ninewells Hospital and now appreciate the life-saving work that goes on in ICU and the coronary care unit. I didn't know it at the time but due to the COVID-19 pandemic and the numbers of patients that required to be admitted to ICU and HDU, other areas of Ninewells had been commandeered and repurposed as additional ICU units. ICU2 was opened due to the numbers of patients requiring intensive care as a result of COVID-19. The main ICU area (ICU1) had been kept reserved for non-COVID-19 patients who required an ICU bed, for example stroke patients, those with severe trauma and patients recovering from life-saving surgery, whilst the additional ICU2 had earlier been designated for COVID-19 patients who required ICU input and had cleared the virus as evidenced by a negative test.

By this point, there were fewer COVID-19 patients in the hospital and ICU2 had been closed to allow some emergency and urgent operating to continue as normal. ICU3 was opened in the Day Surgery recovery area and was designated as 'red' and had the potential to take positive cases. When told that I was to be put in ICU3, Amanda was furious and argued with the medical staff that after all that I had gone through, this could kill me. Amanda later admitted to being dysregulated during her discussion with the medical team. Although she was loyal to the Aberdeen team for having retrieved me and getting me to this point and did not want the medical team to change, the doctors counselled her that this was a normal emotion. The doctors could not offer any alternative and I was given a bed in ICU3. What was yet to come was not known to the medical and nursing staff. They were used to patients emerging from a coma but what condition would I be in? The saying goes, 'Your darkest hour is only 60 minutes long,' mine had been 50 days.

Amanda and the family, particularly John, my elder doctor brother, had discussed the post-coma question at length and knew that many survivors of an ICU stay have organ and/or cognitive damage - the likelihood increasing with the length of a coma. In my case, this would be even greater due to the ECMO and the COVID-19 virus. Nobody could predict the next stage. It was once more a waiting game.

———————————

CHAPTER 7

The Wake-up Call

I SPENT around a week in ICU3 before I was aware that I was starting to regain consciousness. I was later told that this was a relatively calm week with regular observations recorded by the nurses and minimal intervention needed from the medical staff. It was a case of watching and waiting. Apparently, I was able to interact with those looking after me although the combination of critical illness and the multitude of drugs prevented me from having any memory of this time. Amanda continued to have regular contact with the medical and nursing teams and was relieved that although I was in ICU, nothing else was going wrong and hoped that this would continue. The nurses were great at arranging a video call each evening for her to see me and talk to me. Sadly though, I could not reply as I was still deep in sleep.

I did not wake up suddenly. It was a gradual process with me drifting closer to 'the surface' then back into a deeper level of unconsciousness. This continued for some time and although my memory is rather hazy, it did not seem unpleasant at all, more of a 'floating existence'. Looking back, there seemed to be a sense of serenity and I was at peace with myself, with COVID and with the world. Perhaps this was a good thing after everything that had gone before. My first sense to start returning was my hearing yet this was very muffled. I was aware of people around me, but I could not see them. It did not concern me that I could not see anything at this point. I was drifting in and out of a combination of consciousness and sleep and I was oblivious to what was going on. I could not make out what they were saying although I was not bothered. In fact, nothing bothered me. I was totally oblivious to the world around me. As time went on, I could hear the radio in the background and there were songs that I could recognise. I seemed to be quite comfortable just lying and listening to the radio. It was soothing and some of the older tunes took me back to being a child in the 1970s. I remember being driven to school by Dad with Terry Wogan being on Radio 2. I didn't appreciate Wogan's sense of humour until I became an adult, but the songs somehow connected me with a relatively happy time where I didn't have a care in the world. It was probably a good thing that I had no recollection of the violent period that my body, mind and soul had just gone through.

As I slowly became more conscious over a period of days, I could hear more and more. The songs on the radio became ever more familiar and I became aware of singing as well as the music. Frighteningly, the world remained dark. When I tried to see, I found myself staring into nothing. Why could I not see anything? I was puzzled. Gradually, I became aware of my surroundings; I was confused and was cold, and eventually became afraid about what was going on around me. I was surrounded by machines making strange noises. What were these machines? Were they there to help me or to hurt me? There were regular beeping noises, other machines whirred, air moved, and fluid flowed. Regularly as clockwork, my lungs would be inflated. By this point, I was able to initiate each breath and the ventilator would boost my weak chest muscles and provide a rush of air Sometimes I would cough. And boy, did that hurt. A cold blast of air would flash across me chilling my face. I did not know where this was coming from except that it was above me. Every 15 minutes, the blood pressure machine inflated the cuff and squeezed my arm and whilst it was by no means uncomfortable, I wondered what was going on. Periodically, I would retch and sometimes vomit. I would start to hear voices coming close to me. *Who are these people?*

Although my eyes gradually started to be able to identify shapes, I could not see properly for although my glasses had travelled back to Dundee, they were safely in their case. I could not work out why everything around me was fuzzy. The 'floaty' feeling was gone and was replaced with a bit of hard reality. The world seemed more tangible. Yet I was alone, helpless and had no idea where I was. I felt locked-in and had no memory of anything including the previous 50 days, and this has not returned since. I did not have any memories. Indeed, my brain could only focus on the present, not the past and definitely not the future. I did not know if I was paralysed or not as I was hooked up to so many machines: the ventilator, nasogastric tube and the various tubes for body secretions - I couldn't move. Although my hands were free, there were boots on my feet. They were as heavy as lead. There was also a drip going into my arm providing fluids and other drugs. Trying to move was impossible and required such an effort. It seemed futile. I was tired and the fatigue meant that I would drift in and out of sleep.

The ICU3 unit was the recovery suite for the Day Surgery operating theatres and as a result there were no windows. The nurses kept the lights subdued to avoid hurting my eyes. This meant I had to strain my eyes to see. Although I could see shapes, whatever I looked at seemed to move with the walls constantly shifting in and out. It was like being on the ghost train at the funfair. Were the people real or were they part of the scene? I did not know what was going on. I could not remember anything, who I was or why I was there. The doctors and nurses asked me my name periodically, but I could not remember it. For some reason, this did not concern me. I would just try to smile. *What was my name and why was I not annoyed at myself for not knowing it? Was this all a dream or a nightmare?*

And then, one day, I realised that I was in a hospital. I understood that the people who had been floating around me were in fact the nursing staff. As they worked around they told me what they were doing; none of it made any sense. They sometimes asked if I was sore, but I could not speak due to the tracheostomy tube. When I tried to say yes, no sound came out. I tried to signal with my hand. It wouldn't move. I was completely unable to communicate. My thoughts were simplistic, all I could think of was breathing. It took me back to being a small child and wondering how I would remember to breathe while sleeping. A memory of breathlessness flashed through my mind. Was this a real memory or something my mind had made up? I didn't know. Confusion reigned. And then the ventilator would breathe again for me, slowly inflating my lungs with the, oh so precious oxygen that had felt so hard to come by as I went into hospital.

Random thoughts flew through my mind. They were all unconnected and I couldn't make sense of them. All I could hear was the muffled sound of the machines, voices and music. My hearing was not normal and yet it was consistently the strongest of my senses. I had no sense of smell or taste. My fingers and toes had no sense of touch. My neck was itchy from the tracheostomy strap securing the tube in my neck. I was desperate to scratch my neck and try as I might my hand would not move. I felt defeated. There was nothing to do except look at the ceiling for hours on end. Repeatedly, an icy blast of air would flow over me, chilling me to the bone.

I continued to recognise songs played on the radio. This was soothing and comforting and helped with the monotony. It also helped me connect somehow with the world around me. Every news bulletin carried the story of the George Floyd police murder in the USA. I had no idea who George Floyd was or why his story had become so prominent, I nonetheless understood the facts of the story. He had been killed by police in Minneapolis. Even to my disordered brain, this was terrible. I was confused about reports of the Black Lives Matter movement and although I could connect this to the George Floyd murder, I did not have a full understanding of the situation. Every time I fell asleep, the story became larger than life and utterly terrifying. I imagined I was reliving George Floyd's murder, vividly and horribly. I was George Floyd and was lying on the street. The nurses were the police trying to kill me and the tracheostomy tube was a knee on my neck. In my nightmare, I would be shouting out for help whilst dying on the street. Nobody would come to my rescue. It was traumatising and it happened each time I slept. The nurses rolled me every two hours to prevent pressure sores and each time I would try and fight them off. Indeed, the nurses had to restrain me to prevent me from harming them or myself. I would wake up troubled and at times in tears. With no method of communication, I could neither apologise to the nurses nor explain what was going on in my mind. It was horrific and I would fight sleep as I knew what was coming.

I suffered other episodes of paranoia. When awake and looking at the ceiling, I could recall one of the clinic rooms in the dental hospital which has a magnificent painting of various animals on the ceiling to distract children from their treatment. These became real animals amassed on the ceiling above me. There were gorillas and monkeys, bats and snakes. Whenever I drifted off to sleep, they would climb down from the ceiling and torment me, particularly the monkeys. I would try to reach out to catch them, but my hands would not move. The monkeys laughed at me while the bats sniggered at each other. A huge python continually slithered down hissing with its tongue and wrapping itself around my chest compressing my ribcage. It felt slippery and was by no means friendly. I was helpless and frustrated that I could not move away from it. The python restricted my breathing, and I was angry. All I wanted to do was to breathe and it seemed so unfair. I reasoned with myself that it was going to kill me though if I kept breathing, I could beat it. Little did I know that several months later, I would still be troubled by the metaphorical python still restricting my breathing. I kept wanting to ask the nurses to take the animals away. If only I could speak.

The nurses and doctors spoke to me as they worked around me. *But who was I?* I was constantly monitored, and my blood tested. I felt comfortable with all of this even though I had no real idea what was going on. Eventually the penny dropped, and I realised I was pretty unwell. The hospital environment was fairly familiar to me from being on clinic, going to the ward, and occasionally to the operating theatre. *But which hospital was I in?* At this point, I had no memory of going into the induced coma and even if I had, I was waking up in a different part of the hospital with different staff. The doctors and nurses continued to ask me questions and eventually, I remembered my name. I then started to work out other pieces of personal information, my birthday, my wife's name, and other names in the family and so on. I knew fairly swiftly that there was something missing. I did not know what this was. I kept trying to speak yet nothing came out. The nurses had a whiteboard and a felt pen but I couldn't hold the pen to write. Regular as clockwork, at morning ward round, the doctors tried to explain something about my journey, but none of the information made sense to me.

On day 63, a speech and language therapist came to see me. She brought a simple communication aid: an alphabet letterboard on which I could spell simple words. This was marvellous. I could now engage with those around me. Even nodding or shaking my head before this was out of the question as the presence of the tracheostomy tube meant that any head movement was painful. Trying to spell simple words with the letterboard took an age. Anything complicated was just impossible, either there would be some confusion and the spelling became a disaster or I would become too tired to continue. I was angry at myself for failure, however small, so to begin with restricted use of the letterboard to write 'name', 'cold', 'pain', 'drink' and 'sleep'. It was good to spell out my name, as it was part of my identity. Spelling my name helped me start the journey of rebuilding myself.

I was constantly cold and eventually realised that the air swooshing across my face and body periodically was the mechanical ventilation duct above my bed. Every 15 minutes or so, it would send out an icy blast. Was this the python I wondered? The staff did not feel cold although I was constantly frozen. I realised that I was immobile whereas the staff were constantly on the move. I had felt chilled as I fell ill and wondered if this was connected in any way. I started to connect with falling sick and wondered why I was in this part of the hospital having been anaesthetised elsewhere. More blankets were the order of the day and the regular staff got to know that I needed several to keep in the little warmth that I had in bed. I am not the sort of guy who wears shorts in the middle of winter or a T-shirt when walking the dog, rather the opposite in that I prefer to be too warm. I missed our log fire at this point and wondered when I would see it again. 'Pain' was a frequent call, and the nurses would give me a shot of something to help. I am not normally troubled by pain so the feeling of constant pain in my neck, hands, arms, legs and feet was new to me. I was annoyed by this and was frustrated that it was trying to control me rather than my usual response of getting on with life and taking an ibuprofen or paracetamol, or even a wee whisky if needed.

I had some other, less troubling dreams. One dream involved me becoming inadvertently involved in the Brink's Mat robbery of 1983. For some reason I was at Heathrow Airport that day and in my dream I was an adult although I would only have been aged 13 at the time of the robbery. I was threatened with an iron bar by the robbers and was forced to put on a balaclava and go with them while £26 million in gold bullion, diamonds and cash was stolen from a warehouse belonging to Johnson Matthey Bankers. In my dream the nurses were the robbers and had threatened me with certain death if I ever uttered a word to anyone. I was scared that I had now disclosed their identity and not only would my life be in danger but those of my family as well. Another dream related to the next village to us in rural Perthshire and even though we live in the lowlands, the next valley had been turned into a ski resort with alpine conditions for the whole winter. In my mind the skiing was wonderful. The only problem I endured was that the local bus from our house constantly became snowbound as it was not suited to the conditions. Finally, I was experiencing a dream where the nurses were not either trying to harm me or kill me. It was a tremendous relief.

Even though I was extremely swollen and bloated due to my blood vessels being so 'leaky' and my arms, legs, abdomen and face resembling that of a Sumo wrestler, I would wake up each morning very thirsty or as we say in Scotland, with a 'drouth'. This was partially from a water imbalance in my body and also due to the dry air circulating. Initially, the nurses gave me water to sip although it felt gloopy as my mouth was not reacting normally and as time went on, Amanda was able to deliver more exciting things to drink. I enjoy Scottish tap water, but my sense of taste was abnormal, and I craved fizzy juice with flavour. It had to be sugar-free of course as I have been programmed to avoid sugar from my early days at university. Each mouthful was bliss, with the carbonated bubbles cutting through the dryness and mucus in my mouth. The feeling was so refreshing and enjoyable. It is the simple things in life that can be the most effective and this was one example. With the nasogastric tube and the tracheostomy in place, each swallow was painful. I could feel the discomfort right down my oesophagus and there was, therefore, a trade-off between addressing thirst and this most unpleasant sensation. This has remained etched in my mind many months later and I wonder if it will ever leave me.

'Sleep' was an easy request and all that was involved was reclining the back of the bed slightly and turning the lights down. As a respiratory patient, I was not allowed to lie flat in case to minimise the risk of ventilator associated pneumonia even though I also wondered if any fluid or secretions would slip into my lungs and choke me. I got used to sleeping inclined. I would signal with my hand that I wanted my teeth to be brushed every night as well as part of the morning routine and would rarely go to sleep without this being carried out. My mouth didn't feel right, and I soon realised that I needed to floss my teeth. *When was this done last, I wondered?*

Somehow my body had won the critical illness battle, yet I knew I was in a bad way physically, emotionally and psychologically. The hospital staff gradually explained to me what had happened as I became more lucid and able to understand the situation I was in. They let me know me where I was, why I was in ICU3 and the series of events that had brought me to this point. This was difficult to understand initially, and I would get upset when being told that I had been so close to death so many times. I needed to hear little bits of the story from different people to start piecing together some of the events in my head. The majority of the staff were excellent and provided me with this information in a compassionate way. I appreciated their empathy and recognised they were doing their best to help me come to terms with the situation. After all, I had been so close to death on so many occasions, they had run out of options so many times and had to speak to Amanda daily about how grim the situation was.

I came to realise that it must have been horrendous to have witnessed a relatively young patient moreover, a colleague deteriorate so quickly and helplessly. By this time, all my family, friends and colleagues knew what had happened and where I was. Although hospital visiting was banned, many of my hospital colleagues wanted to come to visit me yet were turned away by the staff since I was so weak. This was certainly the right thing to do when I was so easily fatigued. Every ounce of energy was required to be channelled towards recovery. It could not be 'used' for social visits and calls. I reluctantly accepted this fact. Not that I could argue anyway as it was a government edict.

The nurses were tremendously supportive and took time to look after my physical and emotional needs. I would burst into tears spontaneously at times for no reason. I could not control my emotions and this was troubling. I appreciated one of the nurses leaning over me at one point - it could have been day or night - and clasping my hand in hers before telling me that I was 'safe'. This was so important to me and gave me a great degree of reassurance that I was not in any danger. It was such a simple gesture, but it was also so powerful. It still resonates with me many months down the line. Indeed, the nurses would spend lots of time with me telling me the series of events in different ways. I had many questions about the previous two months and did not know where to start. Hearing different versions of the story from different nurses who had all been on duty at different points along the way was very helpful. I was by now, looking for answers, even though I could not speak.

Some of the nurses were so kind and helpful that I would miss them when they finished their shift. One nurse, Niall, was constantly thinking about how he could break the boredom for me. He would search endlessly for the sport on the hospital tablet and set this up to amuse me. He worked out that his personal sports subscription service would work on a hospital computer and duly organised for me to watch various sports. Furthermore, he found out the football club I support, St Johnstone, a relatively small club, based in Perth, Scotland, and asked them for a card. He was delighted to present me with a 'Get Well' card from the football club, signed by the manager, and along with it they had sent some photos of the players. It was touching. Another nurse, Martyn, had been redeployed to ICU3 along with so many other staff and he would help me get comfortable in bed. He always volunteered to speak to the chef in the main kitchen to get me things that I could eat with a tracheostomy tube in place. He would ask for smooth and sloppy items and never disappointed. He would help feed me and had the patience of a saint. Martyn was a golfer and told me about his last round every time he had been on the course. I felt a connection with the outside world somehow just by listening to him. I don't think he ever knew how important his golf stories were to me.

One of my other ICU3 nursing heroes was Gary. I knew from the first time I heard his voice that he had been a local radio DJ many years ago but couldn't ask him as I had the tracheostomy in place. Nobody seemed to mention this to him, and I wondered if it was no longer of interest or was I just getting to an age where these sorts of facts did not matter to the younger generation. How sad I thought. Here was a man who had been prominent in the local media, hosting the breakfast radio show for many years and nobody talked about it. More worryingly, I couldn't talk about it as I was mute. How frustrating. Nonetheless, Gary was delightful. My welfare and comfort were his number one focus every shift. Nothing was ever an issue and he smiled all shift, every shift. He looked after me impeccably and is destined to be one of the best nurses, ever. He would update me on his family, and although I had never met them, it was a loose connection with my own wife and children who I longed to spend time with. Gary helped me enormously with the isolation of being in ICU.

I continued to wonder what was going on and what had happened to me. *Why was I in a subdued hospital ward? What had happened? Which hospital was I in?* These questions would circle in my mind continually. Being told that I had been so close to dying on several occasions was hard to cope with. I wondered if my family knew that I had nearly died and everything was fuzzy. *Where were my family? Could I see them? Had they caught this disease as well? If they had, did they all survive?* I had no news about them and wondered what was going on. I felt so guilty that I hadn't been in contact with them. There were so many questions and worries on my mind. I could not ask any of them.

———————————

CHAPTER 8

More Intensive Care

ONE DAY, the pieces of information fell into place like a jigsaw. I regularly use the jigsaw metaphor at work and in my own life. My brain works in images and is pictorial in nature. Amanda on the other hand thinks in words and is highly schooled in languages. I respect the differences in types of memory and thinking. I have often wondered what it would be like to think using music. Does one see the notes as in a music score or do the sounds and melodies energise the soul to produce a variety of feelings. Good music engages the soul whilst bad music assaults the emotions. Amanda had mentioned to the nursing staff in Aberdeen and Ninewells that one of my favourite singers is Andrea Bocelli and his music was duly played on many occasions.

I could see the issues I had with breathing before coming into hospital and remembered coming in and out of hospital on two occasions - I was latterly told it was three occasions - and being on the ward, deteriorating and having to be anaesthetised. That was it. I had no other memory of the preceding weeks and how I had arrived in this part of the hospital. *Would this memory every return? Would I want this memory to ever return?* I did not know the answer to these questions but knew that now was not the time to fight for these answers. There might be bad news to learn about as well and I wondered if I was being protected. Keeping alive was more important so I continued to focus on breathing as the ventilator helped me re-inflate my lungs.

As time went on, the days became more predictable with a clear distinction between night and day. Each day had a pleasant repetitiveness like in the film *Groundhog Day* and would start in the morning with the nursing handover around 7.40am. I knew that the nightshift nurses had work to do through the night and was aware of them working around my bed in the darkness. It felt like being on a plane at times with a general background noise that is difficult to shut out but is best ignored for a good sleep. Some nights were quiet, others noisy. It was their 'daytime' after all and I tried to accept this. By now, I had found that having the radio playing through the night helped prevent further nightmares and although I would hear the music on awakening through the night, and in particular every two hours when the nurses changed my sleeping position, it was a relief that I was no longer fighting the nurses and felt more settled and well-slept each morning.

If I was awake at handover time either in the morning or evening, the nurses would come and wish me well, which was delightful. As the dayshift team got organised, the relative peace of the night gradually receded, disturbed by the switching on of lights. The first thing they would do is decide who would be administering drugs and who would be doing the checks and adjustments to the equipment, particularly the ventilator. Tubing was changed daily and areas where water vapour had condensed were drained. Settings were tweaked and everything cleaned. The same would be done as the night shift got into gear. On occasion, the neck-strap securing the tracheostomy tube was removed along with the dressing. This provided much needed freedom and I would immediately ask a nurse to scratch my neck. Relief was short-lived as a new neck-strap and dressing was applied. By eight o'clock every morning, the morning drugs had been dispensed.

When I initially regained consciousness, I was on a large cocktail of drugs for various issues: pain, blood pressure, poor sleep, mental health and depression, dizziness, anxiety, nebulisers to help me breathe more easily and creams for various fungal ailments in sensitive areas of my body. Initially these were crushed and administered through the nasogastric tube or intravenous line. It was like being in a chemistry laboratory with exactly the right amount of water being used to make each solution.

As well as being used for drugs, the nasogastric tube was used to feed me. The feed would be changed twice per day in the morning and evening. Initially, I had no idea about this but as my sense of smell started to return, I became aware of how foul the liquid feed smelt. It was disgusting, particularly if it leaked or if I vomited it back up. It reminded me of tomato fertiliser. My mind rushed to thoughts of being in a medical greenhouse.

As the weeks went on, I became able to tolerate swallowing medicines and there would be around 25 different liquids, capsules and tablets to be administered or swallowed. They looked much bigger than they were when in the little medicine pots. I would do my best to take these as quickly as possible but was frustrated on many days as I would vomit them back up. This caused chaos as the nursing staff would be unsure what remained inside and what had been brought up. I felt guilty but the problem could not be helped. I was therefore administered an anti-emetic - either an injection or a tablet - when I could feel the nausea building. I tried to control this as best I could to make everyone's morning less unpleasant. I had no desire to be sick and it drained me first thing in the morning. Drugs would be distributed at various times during the day, but luckily these were much reduced when compared to the early morning round and by the evening, there were again various medicines to be taken both around the start of the nightshift and at 10pm when the lights were generally dimmed for the night.

The enthusiasm of the whole ICU team and their interest in me and my recovery, no matter what time of day, never failed to amaze me. The morning routine was taken up by the serious aspects of the day, with a more relaxed approach in the afternoons and a great deal of flexibility in the evening. The daily routine was helpful in getting me used to a structured day. The next section of the weekday morning began around 9am with Sophie, the team leader for critical care physiotherapy, coming into ICU to find out how the patients had been overnight. She was sensitive to our needs and knew how ill I had been. Sophie was a constant throughout my journey and would greet me with a beaming smile every morning.

From ICU, Sophie would go around the hospital to see her patients and then return for the ICU ward round, which took place around 9:30am. Sophie and the rest of the wider rehabilitation team have the enthusiasm, knowledge and experience to rival anyone who works in the NHS. I often wondered if the rehabilitation role requires a certain disposition or whether this comes with the training. I resolved that it would be a bit of both. Sophie would gather all the information at her preliminary ward round and suggest what was likely to happen during the day. Since my head was initially very confused, it was good to hear information on more than one occasion. I appreciated this tremendously.

On many occasions, Sophie would essentially take the lead on the ward round and the consultants, whilst being exceptionally knowledgeable about drugs, vital signs, treatments, prognosis of certain conditions and so on, would look to Sophie for the answer to how patients were getting on. The ICU consultants, junior doctors, allied health professionals, pharmacists and nurses seemed to enjoy the collegiality of the ward round and it was great to see people being happy at work. It was a chance for them all to catch up with various members of the team about all sorts of small queries, and of course to share information that is vital in ICU. Sometimes, the ward round seemed to be a cast of thousands and on other days, just the core staff. I was no stranger to this as we sometimes have more healthcare professionals and students on a clinic than patients and whilst it is daunting for many patients, I was able to cope with this. The consultants demonstrated an air of respectful authority at this point of the day but at no time did I witness any belittling behaviour. Quite the opposite, in fact, they were exceptionally inclusive and thorough with their bedside manner and teaching. By this point in the first wave, there were, however, only two patients in ICU3 as all others had been discharged, me and an older gentleman, Robin. He had sadly contracted COVID-19 at age 66 and after a spell on a ventilator, had fortunately survived. With only two patients in ICU3, it was hard for the staff not to make friendships with both Robin and me. We were not going anywhere quickly due to our significant rehabilitation needs, and both had a story that seemed astonishing.

Each ward round was fairly swift with an update on the preceding night from the junior doctors and nurses and the medical plan for the day ahead agreed. Some days, the plan was fairly similar to that of the preceding day, nonetheless the consultant managed to present this to me as a step forward. I reckoned eventually that even on the days when there was little to report at the ward round, this was not a step backwards, particularly as I discovered what medical disasters had happened in the weeks before. In addition, medication was reviewed and changes made as needed. The medical/ventilator and rehabilitation objectives for the day ahead were agreed and Sophie informed the medical staff about the physical activities to be undertaken later in the morning. I looked forward to seeing the wider team each day. One question I was asked frequently was, 'Who is the Prime Minister?'. I had no idea at this point who was running the country. I had forgotten that it was the illustrious Boris Johnson and had no idea that the real reason was to test my cognition. The ward round had a more relaxed approach at weekends and although everyone was profess-ional, it helped me recognise when the weekend had arrived and that there would be less of a planned routine. This was somewhat comforting even as I was recovering from critical illness.

Over the initial weeks while I was recovering in ICU, the junior doctors were part of the ward round; I was familiar with this approach from my days as a junior. Everyone huddled round the notes trolley and although there were subtle differences between how each consultant ran the ward round, it was the opportunity for the juniors to present the patient they had been looking after to the consultant and ask questions not only for answers to benefit the patient's care but also for learning. I remember being asked by a surgical professor on a teaching ward round, 'The patient goes to the toilet lots at night. What is the diagnosis?'. I had remembered this occasion many times over the years particularly as none of the juniors knew the answer. I still don't know the answer, but I suspect it might be Type II Diabetes. He was encyclopaedic. This professor was the most gifted surgeon and when anyone was in trouble surgically, he would be the person to call. I knew that medical leadership is not only about age, but experience, knowledge and most importantly, wisdom. Wisdom is difficult to teach and indeed to learn, being part of a functional team is an excellent place to start. The combined wisdom within the ICU team was reassuring and I knew that the whole team would do everything needed to ensure all the patients received the best possible care both medically and mentally.

If chest physiotherapy was needed to help clear my lungs of fluid, Sophie would undertake this at the end of the ward round. I had heard of chest physiotherapy before but did not know much about it. Sophie was focused on ensuring I would have clear lungs every day. At this point, my lungs were very weak both in terms of their ability to deal with any debris and my diaphragm and chest muscles had wasted away with the ventilator having done so much of their work. Looking back, it is not surprising that I was not able to deal with any fluid adequately. Whilst I did not look forward to chest physiotherapy, I accepted that it was an essential part of the treatment. Sophie would place one hand on each side of my sternum and press extremely hard for one minute, repeated several times until I violently coughed up what seemed vast quantities of viscous mucus, with the remainder being suctioned through the tracheostomy tube using a catheter which rasped my trachea raw. Some days, I would cough so much that my eyes were bloodshot for the rest of the day. It was horrible to have to undergo this day after day, but I knew it was necessary. I can still feel the various sensations of my breathing being restricted and my ribs being pushed inwards due to the pressure, and my trachea being sore afterwards to this day. I often wondered if this is what people with cystic fibrosis have to go through on a daily basis. I acknowledged that this treatment would hopefully be temporary, and I was only too quick to be thankful for this fact. Moreover, I could breathe more easily once my lungs had cleared. I was exceptionally grateful for this.

The nurses continued to pamper me like a baby. Never have I been so well looked after in my life. The nurses would give me a bedbath at around 10.30am and would change the bed sheets. It involved being cleaned from head to toe and once dry, being rolled from side to side to remove and replace the bed sheets. The nurses seemed to undertake this with a degree of pleasure at being tactile with me as a patient and I began to get a feel for each nurse's individual technique and order for doing things. One of the nurses, Matt, had an excellent technique. He would place towels around each area to be cleaned, would use warm water and stroke the soapy wipe in the same direction along my arms and legs. I appreciated the high temperature of the water, since my thermal regulation was not working properly at this point and the cleansing technique was strangely relaxing on my skin which did not have a normal sense of touch. Each area of my body would be patted dry, rather than being rubbed and then covered up. Great care was taken not to disturb any of the lines or cables attached to me and the nurses seemed to take a degree of satisfaction in the tactile aspect of the bedbath ritual in order to make me comfortable. I was frequently offered moisturising cream for the lower half of my legs and feet and although I have not had a proper massage in my life, this was tremendous. Not only was the skin of my legs and feet extremely dry, but they were very pale. Indeed my whole body was pale - my legs were pure white. As they were massaged, some colour would return, and I would be grateful for the time that the team would invest in improving the circulation going down to my toes even though I couldn't feel them.

The magical chest of drawers would be opened and various lotions and bottles to pamper me would be produced. The nursing staff would often smell the contents and remark to their co-worker that the contents smelled lovely. The downer was that I still couldn't smell a thing. I could now hear, see, and had a degree of sensation on the skin of my thorax and abdomen but could not smell or taste anything. How odd, I thought, but accepted this as at that point, I knew no different. At that point each day, the stickers for the ECG leads were renewed and my gown changed. It felt agreeable to be clean and having my teeth brushed was a treat. How I looked forward to this each morning and evening just to get my teeth brushed.

My mouth did, however, feel nauseating and I longed to floss my teeth. There was no chance of flossing my teeth as my hands did not work properly. I worried about the damage that would happen to my gums if I was not able to floss for many months, or evermore. Sure, I appreciated a degree of angst about this was an occupational hazard, but it was there nonetheless. One of Sophie's daily tests was to get me to touch my chin, nose and head. Initially, I was lucky not to poke out an eye, so I realised flossing my teeth was out of the question. I couldn't summon the energy to ask the nurses initially using the communication board either. In addition, my jaw joints were sore, and my tongue had a strange continual burning sensation. I thought this might have been linked to the aches and pains throughout my body, but I wasn't sure. At this point in the journey, my feet had been suffering from what is known as footdrop, where my ankles were not able to hold my feet up in bed. I was provided with different types of boots to keep my ankles flexed and reduce the strain on my feet, which were painful. There were also cuffs for my calves that inflated periodically to stop any prospect of a further deep vein thrombosis from occurring. I did not want to run from the risk of one of these forming again, breaking off and travelling round my bloodstream to my lungs and endangering my life. The boots meant that any change in position in the bed required a significant effort for the nursing staff to take these off each time I needed rolled. It was great to have the boots removed just to let my feet breathe from time to time but oh, how my ankles ached if my feet were not captured and re-booted for any period of time. I was numb from my elbows to my fingertips and from my hips to my toes. I had no idea someone was touching these areas unless I could see what was going on. *How strange I thought, why was this?*

I was unaware that the physiotherapists had also been coming to ICU to see me from day one. As recovery progressed, the occupational therapists also joined the rehabilitation team looking after me. The physiotherapists and occupational therapists undertook muscle and joint mobilisation daily and had tried to keep the physical aspects of my body working as best they could. The therapistsphysiotherapists arrived at 11am, and while I was bedbound, they mobilised my joints and started to help me regain the ability to lift my arms and legs which seemed like massive progress. Even lying in bed and having my arms and legs mobilised was exhausting initially. Each of the physiotherapy team finished their session with putting me back under the blankets and putting the boots back on to stop foot-drop. Their final act of kindness, every time, without fail, was to ask me if there was anything else they could do before leaving me. How sweet. I knew I was in caring hands. Physiotherapists are for some reason also called physio-terrorists and looking back on my time, I am minded that this is extremely unfair. The occupational therapists also spent considerable time with me with a clear aim to help me use my hands for basic functional tasks initially, such as eating and drinking.

For many hours when on the ventilator and on many occasions, I could think of nothing else except my breathing, wondering if it would always be laboured or if it would improve. Oh, how I wanted it to improve; my thoughts turned frequently to trying to help my brain and body work together towards this aim. The doctors repeatedly told me that they didn't have any information from previous patients who had been affected by COVID-19 and there was no information they could give me about prognosis. This was frustrating, but I appreciated that it was also frustrating for the medical team. By this point in the pandemic in Scotland, it had been pointed out to me by the doctors that I was the most severely affected COVID-19 patient they had treated who had survived. They were puzzled but nevertheless delighted that I had managed to stay alive despite so many close shaves with death. However, this meant that I was an outlier and any information they had for 'Mr Average' would not have been relevant to me since my pattern of disease and recovery was different. I resigned myself to this point early on and therefore made sure any positive news never became exaggerated in my mind. The negatives remained: there was talk at one point of the possibility of a lung transplant if my lungs did not recover sufficiently; this was hard to take on board.

The ICU medical and nursing staff were incredible. They not only monitored me ~~very~~ closely and catered for every need, but also treated me aggressively for a further pseudomonas lung infection. I was disappointed at this setback having fought so hard to breathe over the previous weeks. By adding a strong antibiotic to the nebuliser the pseudomonas was eradicated. I had heard of pseudomonas before and Annabelle, the dear elderly mother of Amanda's friend, Julia, had had a battle with these bacteria over many years, in addition to her cystic fibrosis. I wondered how she was doing and hoped she hadn't been unlucky enough to contract COVID-19. All I had to do was to breathe the antibiotics in. I struggled with breathlessness and on many occasions required various salbutamol and saline nebulisers just to be able to get enough oxygen into my lungs. The fluids for these would be poured into a reservoir in the tubing and I would breathe as much as I could. Sometimes they helped and at other times they seemed to have no effect. Breathing still seemed to take up so much time and energy.

Whilst I could not speak due to the tracheostomy and continued to rely on the alphabet board to communicate, I was becoming more cognitively aware as the days rolled on. I could now spell some more advanced words and phrases such as, 'How are you?', 'Turn up the lights please' and 'Change of position please'. I knew the ICU staff were looking after me very well but my voice could not be heard literally or figuratively. *How long would I be silenced?* It was then that I started to wonder if my voice would be okay and whether my voice would sound the same if it ever returned. I also kept wondering who was this guy Dominic Cummings that the radio news reports kept referring to and why he had travelled to Durham for an eye test. *Why was this on the news I wondered?*

I had some crazy dreams and looking back on them now, I am minded they were grounded in fact. One night, I dreamt that I had pulled out the ECMO lines in my neck and groin. Blood rushed everywhere and covered the bed in scarlet red. The team worked furiously to stop the flow and eventually succeeded. I wondered what all the fuss was about. On another occasion, I had a dream that I did not want to have the flexi-pipe in my bottom for faeces anymore and simply removed it. No fuss. Strangely, all of these lines had been removed under deep sedation before I started to regain consciousness and at no point did I have any 'awake' knowledge that these had been in place. I knew people sometimes have memories of staff conversations when they are having operations. I was now joining the group of patients who could remember happenings. It was all rather strange.

I had other dreams about the hospital. One night I dreamt that I had to get back to work and somehow I managed to convince one of the nurses that I needed to be discharged and, with some persuasion, I picked up my car keys and drove home. I woke up with a jolt. There was no chance of me even being able to walk so this was far from the truth. On another occasion, I was convinced that I was still in HDU and having disconnected the ventilator and lines myself to go to the bathroom, I had got into the empty bed next to mine. I remember arguing with the nurses later that night that I wanted to use the commode, as I disliked the bedpan and the need for it to be cleaned by the nursing staff. A frequent daytime thought I had was that I was totally convinced I had booked a holiday and I didn't want to miss it. I needed to get access to my phone to see our favourite airline app. However, I couldn't remember the PIN for my phone. How frustrating.

The dream I had had about getting home had scared me. I soon realised that I was not going to be in any fit state to return home for some considerable time. I decided to try to make the most of each day as it unfolded and quickly accepted that this was 'my lot' for the foreseeable future. The lack of communication was frustrating. I could at least supplement the alphabet board words with hand signals, principally thumbs up and down, and facial expressions. I learned to exaggerate these for clear and effective communication. Shaking and nodding my head was extremely unpleasant and would induce extreme nausea. I was aware that the phone would ring just after 8am as the nurses were organising the day ahead and that it would be Amanda enquiring if I had had a good night and it became clear that the nursing team were focussed on providing the family with the best care as well. How reassuring it was to realise that Amanda was being supported through this ordeal.

I was troubled by other delusional thoughts and wild emotional swings with highs from being alive to long periods of low mood, guilt (about the effect of my condition on my family, work colleagues and friends) and frequent thoughts that I could escape from being locked in by stopping breathing. Breathing was such hard work and sapped so much of my energy. It seemed to occupy so much space in my brain. I knew I had to concentrate so much on this key activity, nonetheless, I was tired of having to spend so much time and effort on survival. *Would stopping breathing make everything easier? Could I escape if I didn't put in any more effort? What would happen if I stopped breathing? Would the pain go away? Would I be able to make contact with deceased relatives and in particular, my father who had died when I was so young?* I was tempted to try this out on many occasions. Each time, I would be brought back to normality by either the ventilator re-inflating my lungs or the staff needing to do something for me. I knew that I was emotionally fragile but tried to regain my inner strength on each occasion. How glad I am that I did not give up in this most difficult period. I now dread what effect this would have had on my family. How could I have been so selfish to think that my feelings were more important than anyone else in my family?

I had given up control when I asked to go on CPAP. I now realised I had also surrendered my dignity and part of my identity. I had acknowledged that I was now a long-term hospital patient who had been gravely ill and had narrowly escaped death. What I had yet to learn was the number of times I had been so close to death. I was not in charge of my own destiny and had accepted this. In 49 years of life, I had prided myself at being in control. What could I do now? I couldn't even go to the toilet myself, even this was out of my control with a catheter in place. I tried hard not to show the doctors, nurses and Amanda how frustrated I was. I was down, but not out. I had learned to accept defeat but not to be defeated. I had reached the crossroads point as a long-term patient and now had to choose whether to be a victim, a lucky survivor or to get on and slowly rebuild my life. I didn't sleep well that particular night but vowed with myself the only logical option was to set daily and weekly goals, however small, and to get on with life. It was not going to be easy but how could I give up after everything that everyone had done for me. It would have been a kick in the teeth for them. And I knew just how much damage this could do from professional experience.

Where would I begin? My first goal was simple. Put on my socks. This would have two advantages, firstly they would help keep my feet from feeling like blocks of ice, and secondly, I would have achieved something I hadn't been able to do for months. I spelled out 'socks please' using the alphabet board and the nurses rummaged around my faithful brown holdall bag. I didn't know it was in ICU3 with me. I was somewhat pleased to see it as it travels with me when I go away for clinics where an overnight stay is required and sometimes for meetings and conferences. It was another small connection with my old life which now seemed so distant. Unfortunately, there were no socks in the bag. Luckily the ICU nurses searched the trolley that seemed to be like a Mary Poppins bag. It contained everything from medical equipment to sticky tape, towels to straws, and spare knives and forks. It was amazing to see what could be found in these drawers and I wanted to play a game where I would ask the nurses for items just to see if they were stocked in the drawers. Unsurprisingly, a pair of red socks was produced, and I gestured to the nurses that I would like to put them on. I had no idea where my feet were so ran my hand down my right leg. What a fright I got. Instead of the shin that I would normally feel, all that my hand could sense was a razor-sharp narrow bone and floppy skin. It was a horrible sensation, and I was dejected. I felt my left shin and, if anything, it felt in a worse state. How would I ever stand and walk again if my legs had withered away? With help from one of the nurses, I gradually eased the socks over my feet and up my ankles. It seemed to take forever. I was very satisfied on completion. I had met my first daily goal and fell fast asleep.

PHOTOGRAPHS

SECTION ONE

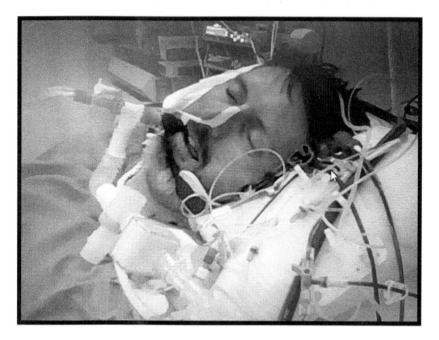

1 — On ECMO with the ventilator tubing going in through my mouth and down into my lungs along with the ECMO blood lines taking blood back and forth through the blood pump and oxygenator, along with the dialysis lines transporting blood to and from the dialysis machine. In the background are all the monitoring devices and out of view to the right is the 'screen' showing all vital signs, which would alarm each time something was not quite right.

2 — One of our good friends recorded a 'mash up' tune he had
compiled for our wedding and recorded it so that it could
be played back to me while in the arms of Morpheus.

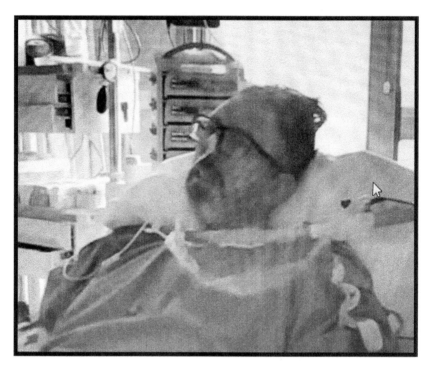

3 — After the tracheostomy was placed (image quality is not good
as Amanda took this as a screenshot from a video call
to remind herself that I was making progress).

4 — The jungle scene from the ceiling of one of the
treatment rooms in the dental hospital.

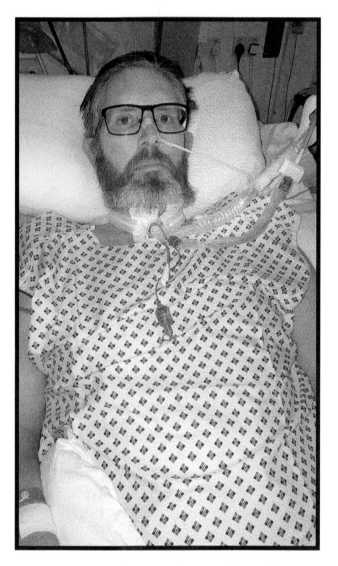

5 — In ICU with the ventilator in place and the
nasogastric tube. My beard and moustache had grown
significantly in the time I was in a coma and was eventually
trimmed by one of the nurses, it was quite a job!

6 — The Get Well Soon card from my football team.

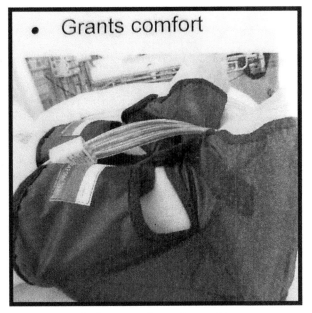

7 — The boots with my feet poking out
at the top of the photograph.

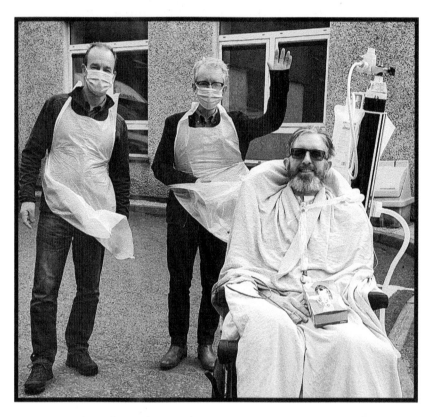

8 — Outside on the ventilator meeting Callum and Douglas (Colin is out of view). The oxygen cylinder would sometimes nearly run out on visits outside necessitating a rather speedy return inside in case the back-up also ran dry.

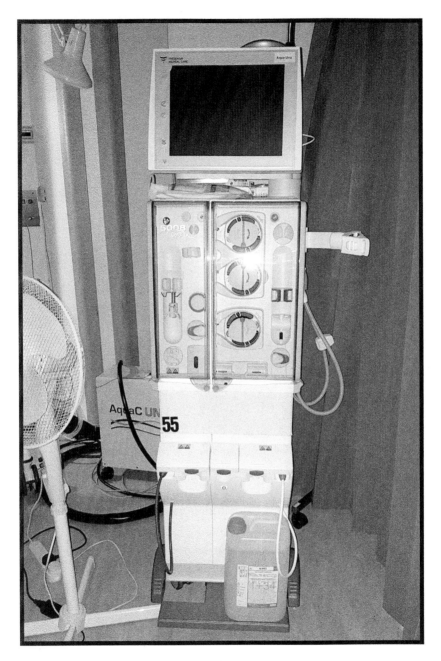

9 — My bedside companion.

through a long and difficult journey since his
admission in March and he has shown amazing
strength of character throughout. We all wish him well
with his continued recovery."

Medical Director Professor Peter Stonebridge added
his well wishes to Grant. He said, "I am so pleased that
Grant has now left the ICU. It is a great step forward
given how unwell he was and I look forward to seeing
him continue to make progress."

YOUTUBE.COM
**'Sickest survivor' of COVID-19 leaves ICU after nearly
three months**

10 — The sickest survivor is discharged from ICU after 128 days.

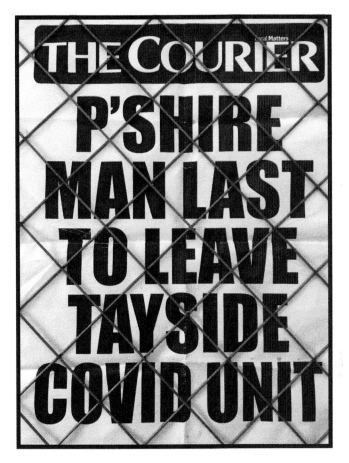

11 — A newspaper board outside one of our local newsagents.

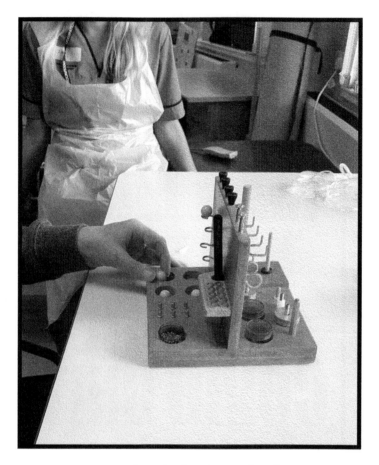

12 — Relearning hand control in the
occupational therapy gym.

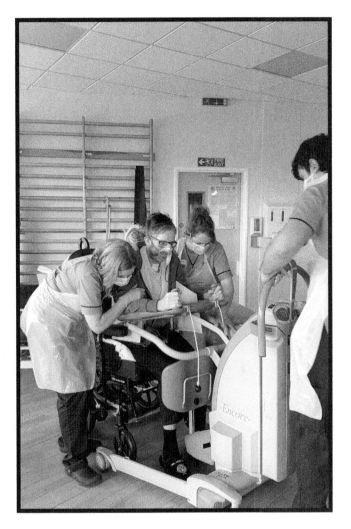

13 — The Stand Aid machine being used to lift me up
in preparation for my first steps.

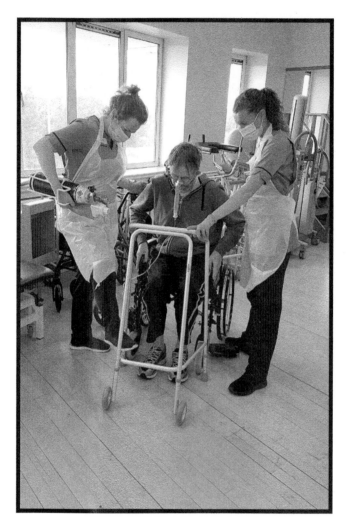

14 — Learning to walk with a Zimmer frame.

15 — Lunch made as part of the kitchen test.
Not quite a Michelin-starred restaurant!

CHAPTER 9

Ventilation

ALTHOUGH ICU3 had no windows, I had decided that it was time for my body and mind to try to distinguish between day and night: day should be busy and night reserved for sleeping. Emotionally I was becoming stronger and acknowledged this. Thankfully, the nightmares, paranoia and delusional thoughts were behind me.

The ICU team understood that I was a long-term patient in a ward with no windows and was disconnected from the world. I had not seen daylight for two months and it was springtime. I realised I had missed a chunk of the year, how much I did not know. The nurses and doctors often commented on the nice weather and I wondered what the outside was like as late spring became early summer.

I was surprised how well I seemed to be coping at being trapped indoors. I knew that I wouldn't be able to survive for many months without reconnecting with the outside world and whilst various countries including the UK were on lockdown, I felt locked-up and to some extent, a prisoner. I didn't know what lockdown meant for the population at large so would ask the nurses what this involved for them on a personal level. The nurses would tell me frequently that their social life and normal activities were curtailed due to the government restrictions that had been put in place. These seemed to be alien to me and to have to queue to enter a shop seemed like something from the Soviet

Union or in some far-flung countries with a failing dictatorship. I had no understanding what the restrictions meant but knew that there would be winners as adversity results in opportunity. I had even remembered the name of the Prime Minister and proudly told one of the consultants on the ward round one day that it was Boris Johnson.

The doctors and physiotherapists told me that the rehabilitation journey would be much longer than the critical illness battle. It was honest information but hard to fathom when my head was not thinking straight. *How long had I been in hospital and how long did they expect the rehabilitation journey to take?* I was also aware that Robin, the other COVID-19 patient in ICU3, was ahead of me in terms of treatment. I wondered if he had been as severely affected as me or if he had come into hospital before me. I couldn't speak and neither could he so there was no point in trying. I knew from conversations and goings on that he was able to be taken outside to meet his wife on one or two occasions. His wife had also turned up one day to deliver something for him and the senior charge nurse, Susie, had encouraged her to come inside to see Robin for a short while.

I hoped that one day, I too could go outside. After all, I had been locked in for some considerable time and I craved the outside world in the same way an alcoholic craves a drink. Susie was an exceptional nurse and I thought this was a fantastic gesture. Susie would talk to me endlessly about other patients she had nursed over the years, and without breaking any confidences or sharing any personal or medical information, she helped me appreciate the spectrum of critical illness and how the staff were able to bend the rules for the sickest patients. I loved the story about the old gentleman who was sadly dying from cancer where the nurses arranged for him to see his dog in the ward one last time before he passed away. How important this must have been for the gentleman and how much fun it must have been for the nurses to smuggle a dog into ICU.

I worked out where I had contracted the COVID-19 virus. It was at work in mid-March and I had being doing a procedure for a patient that involved the generation of a fine aerosol mist and as the patient had an unusual cough (but did not feel unwell), it was likely that I had breathed this now infected air in. I had spent the rest of the morning in the same room and as the windows were closed, I simply breathed in more and more infected air. I would have become infected there and then with a high viral load. I did not feel any malice as the patient in question had no idea that they were spreading the virus. Indeed, I am sure this patient would have been horrified to know that their procedure had resulted in me becoming so heavily infected and critically ill. I felt reassured that I was not angry at what had happened. After all, it was not the patient's fault. It was just bad luck. I was at least alive. As my condition improved, the nursing and medical staff started to speak to me about where I had possibly caught the virus and they all thought it was likely that I had picked it up at work due to the close proximity of an orthodontist's nose and mouth to the patient's airway, even when wearing a fluid repellent mask. In my opinion, it was spending the rest of the morning in the 'infected' room with the window closed that was more important than the procedure itself and everyone generally agreed with me.

I finally remembered the PIN to unlock my phone. It was early one morning and I was pleased with myself for managing to recall it. One of the nurses kindly wrote it down on a sticky label and put this on the front cover of the phone in case I forgot it again. I could now use my own device except there was a problem. My hands and arms were not fully functional and I could not hold it in one hand and type with the other. *What was I going to do?* I wanted to start reconnecting with the outside world so had to find a solution. The rails on the edges of the over-the-bed table could help. If I wedged the phone in the corner and held it in place with one hand, I could type slowly with the other. Result! My phone had been switched off for months but had received many, many messages while I had been offline. I decided that I was not going to be able to go through these quickly and needed time to be able to learn to be comfortable with reading and messaging people again.

The first text was to Amanda. It seemed to take forever to type but I was happy at being able to communicate directly with her, even though the nurses and doctors were only too happy to relay messages between us. There are some conversations that are best done directly, not because they are secretive or silly, but simply because they need to be direct. I knew that having unlocked the phone, I now had the time to text other people but it was so tiring even just texting Amanda that I did not go any further for fear of overload. I could also check my airline app and could confirm that we had not indeed booked a trip to New Zealand just before going into hospital. To this day I do not know where this idea came from. Perhaps it was a dream while I was unconscious for 50 days.

Dr McJoss, one of the consultants, asked me one day if I wanted to go outside to meet Amanda. I was delighted and immediately answered, 'Yes'. What a treat, I hadn't been outdoors for over eight weeks, except to be transferred to and from Aberdeen and that was far from a treat. Little did I know how much effort would be required to make this happen. Going outside was quite an occasion and involved an ICU bed, portable ventilator, a backup oxygen tank, resuscitation equipment, portable suction and several staff to accompany me. I felt a little guilty as there was nothing I could do to help while the staff prepared everything meticulously and double and triple checked they had everything needed in case of any emergency, however small. This all took over an hour. The final task before setting off was to disconnect me in terms of the arterial line and the ventilator tubing from the 'plumbed in' ventilator and connect me to the portable ventilator. The arterial line had a clever transducer chip which connected from my wrist to the ventilator to help with monitoring and I thought this was intelligent medical science. I was clearly very apprehensive about any break in oxygen as I knew my body had been craving oxygen for many weeks and needed an oxygen supply. It was vital to my existence. Dr McJoss ensured I was not in any danger and looked after me so wonderfully. She reassured me that I would feel a little puff in my neck as the ICU ventilator was disconnected and a small surge of air as the portable ventilator was connected but this was nothing to worry about. I knew I was in safe hands.

I was duly transferred over to the portable ventilator and off we went. I will remember this trip for the rest of my life and it ranks highly in the list of important occasions in my existence. The team navigated the bed through doors and along corridors and outside and there waiting, was Amanda. I hadn't seen her in such a long time and I cried. Amanda kept her composure as usual. I couldn't speak due to the tracheostomy and therefore needed help to communicate with the letterboard. Despite the awkwardness of communication, we spent some much-needed time together and as the whole 15-minute experience had tired me out, I was taken back inside. It was also the first time I had felt fresh air on my face for such a long time and it felt refreshing, even though there was a mechanical ventilation duct above my head in ICU3. The difference was that it was warm air outside and it was natural ventilation.

Back indoors, the journey was repeated in reverse and I was reconnected to the main ventilator along with all the various pieces of indoor monitoring equipment. I saw areas of the hospital that I had not been to in my time working there and the outside area I was taken to was an ambulance bay. There were ambulances bringing patients into the hospital and I hoped their journey would be somewhat simpler than mine. It struck me as we went out of the hospital that there were several porters and patients smoking close to the door and, as a respiratory patient who had fought so hard to stay alive on so many occasions, I vowed to do something about this when I was being discharged. My first cousin once removed was one of the ICU doctors and it was lovely for George to be part of the team engineering this very important day for me. I had not been able to properly see him since attending his father's funeral just before I became ill. I knew his family would have wondered if I had contracted COVID-19 at the funeral since it was the last large gathering I had attended in March. This was not where I had picked up the virus. I was delighted that he would finally be able to report to his immediate family that I was well enough to go outside earlier in the day.

Day by day my lungs improved and the ventilator support was incrementally reduced, a process called 'weaning'. I knew this was an essential part of this phase of the journey back to respiratory independence but I was nervous at each step of the way. On most occasions, I noticed this but it did not present any problems, whilst on other occasions, even a minimal change seemed to be impossible to acclimatise to and the ventilator support would need to be increased again. The doctors and nurses knew exactly what they were doing and although I had a rough idea of respiratory physiology from my days at university, I knew they were much more knowledgeable. Daily, my blood gases would be measured from my arterial line and adjustments made accordingly. Positive end expiratory pressure helps to keep the air sacs in the lungs inflated when on a ventilator and is one of the settings that would be adjusted.

I had no real understanding of this but the doctors and nurses assumed I did. It was lovely and reassuring that they thought I was knowledgeable about this! It would only be once I could manage to use my mobile phone properly that I would be able to find out information on the internet relating to this fact. As time elapsed, breathing became slowly easier. This was tremendous and on days where relatively large gains in terms of the ventilator support being reduced were made, I felt delighted. I started to explore the recovery journey in my head and reasoned that my lungs were making progress but wondered if the rest of my body was improving at the same rate. I returned to the earlier conversation about the possibility of a transplant and felt that it would now be consigned to history as I was doing better. A couple of the nurses, however, had mentioned that some respiratory patients require oxygen support at home and a cylinder backpack outdoors. But, of course, COVID-19 was still new to everyone and there was no idea about the prognosis for patients such as me. *Would I need to be attached to an oxygen cylinder on a permanent basis when I got home?* I wondered.

The visits outside continued every few days and on the second occasion, I was hoisted into a reclining chair. It did not have the same level of comfort as the ICU bed and not only was the hoisting process uncomfortable, I was not relaxed in the recliner chair. Nevertheless, this was not going to put me off as waiting outside was Callum, his partner, Douglas and Colin. Again, all the equipment was assembled, I was disconnected from the main ventilator and attached to the portable machine. Again, there was a break in continuity between the two but I was ready this time and it did not seem like a problem. We travelled the same journey outside in the reclined position and I reminded myself of the Monty Python film *The Meaning of Life* where one of the scenes involved a hospital bed being pushed through a series of hospital doors. It was wonderful to see Callum, Douglas and Colin. They had all done so much for me over the previous two months and I wanted to thank them, but I still couldn't speak. Whilst this was tough, I knew there would be another opportunity. It was lovely to be with them and the sun even came out to warm us. My glasses went dark due to the sunshine and one of the nurses said to me they didn't know that I wore this type of glasses. I was curious about other aspects of my life that were hidden from them. Even though I wanted to go outside every day, I realised the inconvenience that this caused the staff and the huge effort required. It also needed a doctor to be present and this would only be possible if there was enough capacity elsewhere in the team.

'DYING TO LIVE'

On the third occasion it was suggested that I go outside, there was a treat in store for me. The doctors had phoned Amanda in the morning as per normal as Sophie, the lead physiotherapist, had suggested that Amanda bring Sherlock Bones for an afternoon visit. Sophie let me know while doing the second of the morning physiotherapy sessions that Sherlock would be coming in at some point. I now can't recall exactly what activity I was doing but the prospect of seeing Sherlock again took my mind off the discomfort. Later in the morning, Sophie returned to ICU with one of her team, each pushing a special wheelchair with extra support at the head, waist and feet. One was for Robin and one for me. The sight of *my* wheelchair brought mixed emotions: whilst it would allow a degree of freedom, it meant that I was now disabled for the foreseeable future. *Would I be able to enjoy golf, skiing, cycling or ride my motorbike ever again?* None of the medical team could tell me if I would be able to do any of these activities in the future. They cautioned me against being too adventurous with my thoughts, which was frustrating, but I understood their reasons.

I kept wondering what one of the machines was beside my bed as I was transferred from the bed to the wheelchair to go outside each time. I could work out the ventilator, which inflated my lungs every fifteen seconds, and the blood pressure/ECG/pulse/ blood oxygen saturation monitor, which would beep and signal that attention was needed on a fairly frequent basis but I was puzzled by the floor-standing machine that had lots of knobs and dials on the front with tubes running along the floor away from me. It made a constant whooshing noise all day and all night and I was perplexed. I asked one of the nurses one day and she said that it was a dialysis machine. I wondered why there was still a dialysis machine beside my bed. I thought this was long behind me but after some discussion I discovered that due to the requirement to dialyse my blood while I was infected with COVID-19, the machine had to remain with me until I definitely no longer needed it and then it would be stripped down for full cleaning. It turned out that the machine had been allocated in case I needed further dialysis on return and as it was plumbed in, it was the machine that had been making the whooshing noise beside me for weeks. The nurse arranged for it to be removed, cleaned and made available for another patient.

Transferring between the ICU bed and the wheelchair required me to be hoisted back and forth. Senior Charge Nurse Susie found a brand new sling for the hoist that would stay with me. The sling was put underneath me and the hoist lifted me like a cocoon, then the bed would be slid out and the wheelchair put underneath and the hoist would lower me into the chair. It was easier to keep the sling in place and wrap me in blankets to keep me warm rather than remove it. This was the first excursion in the new wheelchair and indeed the first time I had sat up for any amount of time. It felt weird to travel looking straight ahead and I was noticeably dizzy but did not want this to spoil the trip. Outside waiting for me was Amanda along with Sherlock Bones. At this point, Sherlock was a 16-month-old yellow Labrador and was still a puppy at heart. I have had a series of Labradors over the years and boy, they have been an important part of family and my life. I appreciate their attributes immensely. Although not the cleverest of dogs, they are exceptionally loyal and have a voracious appetite, a bit like myself. The irony was that I had no real interest in food in ICU and had wondered if my appetite would ever return.

It had been over two months since I had last been at home with Sherlock and he had grown a little. His paws were as huge as I had remembered and he was confused by my scent. I guess I smelled more of a hospital than myself. He was patient and soon realised who I was, but understandably for a young dog, Sherlock was somewhat interested in the accompanying staff and the smells around the hospital entrance. The physiotherapists and OTs were not able to join the afternoon trip outside but saw us from a window above. It was then that I understood why they were so keen for Sherlock to come to visit. They are all animal mad and oh, what trouble I was in on the Monday morning at the ward round. I was told that if Sherlock came again, I was to make sure that they could join in. They left no doubt in my mind. After going back inside, the procedure to get me back to bed seemed more routine. I was disconnected from the portable ventilator and portable monitoring and hoisted back to bed and reconnected to the main ICU systems. It had been a superb day and I was delighted that I had seen both Amanda and Sherlock. I asked if the bed could be positioned at 45 degrees to the wall to avoid the mechanical ventilation vent from being directly above me. What a difference this made and finally I escaped from the icy blast.

Alison, the speech and language therapist, had come into ICU several times to make sure I was managing some communication with the alphabet letterboard. She came in one day carrying a large box and put it down at the end of the bed. I knew it wasn't an empty box but didn't know what was inside. As usual, Alison checked that I was persevering with the letterboard and asked if I was keen to try a different method of communication that might be easier. I instantly tapped out 'yes' on the letterboard. Alison opened the box and brought out an expensive looking tablet with a plug-in keyboard. It was a voicing tablet. She had been able to purchase this from some additional funding and was keen for me to make use of it. Between us, we tried to set it up and got it working, of sorts. I was able to type in some phrases and it would speak them back, in the same manner as Professor Stephen Hawking's voicing computer. Unlike him, it was hoped that I would regain the power of speech so this would be an interim solution for me. It didn't work as Alison had expected and therefore after 45 minutes or so, she took it away and said that she would return in a day or so with it.

The next morning was day 78, and one of the ICU consultants who had met me at the start of the journey was on duty. Dr McLow was the consultant who I had asked to save my life. He asked me how I was feeling and I signalled with a thumbs-up. As per his normal ICU routine, the nursing staff and Sophie were asked for an update on the previous night and the charts were checked. Some minor adjustments to drugs, oxygen and ventilator settings were determined. He then suggested he reduce the pressure in the cuff at the base of the tracheostomy tube on a trial basis as part of the treatment protocol. I had no idea about the treatment protocol but knew as my life had been in exceptional hands, my future care would also be excellent. The nursing team were asked for a small syringe and this was attached to the tube linking to the cuff. I was used to the pressure in the cuff being adjusted and knew when it was leaking as air from the ventilator that it would escape past the cuff into my throat. When this happened, I would signal to the nurses that something was wrong and they would correct it.

The syringe was duly used to deflate the cuff and I shared a truly euphoric moment with the staff by speaking my first words. I was ecstatic. Although my voice was croaky, I was finally able to thank the team for saving my life and could now hold a short conversation with the team close by. Everyone in the department, and I mean everyone was called to witness the event as there had been significant concern that the length of ECMO, length of unconsciousness and the brain haemorrhage could have had an adverse impact on the speech centre in my brain. In the end, there were some 20 people around the bed; the whole team seemed relieved. It ranks as one of the most important days in my life and still makes me emotional even as I write this chapter many months later. Then came the problem. I could now breathe more easily and could speak, but the usual clinical practice involves the cuff being deflated for increasing amounts of time over several days but fully inflated at night. I was adamant that this was time for a protocol deviation, and I got my way. The cuff was left totally deflated during the day and the ventilator tubing was changed to allow me to breathe high-flow oxygen through my nose. Overnight, the cuff was to be re-inflated and although I understood it was for my safety, I knew that I would feel excluded from the world every night. It would, however, feel great to be free from the ventilator during the day from now on.

That evening, the one-way conversations came to an end. I video called Amanda and surprised her with the power of speech. She was amazed and was in tears. I was in tears. She explained to me that the consultants had been concerned about the effect of the long stay on the speech centre in my brain. Amanda had also been worried but had concealed her thoughts from me. Regaining speech was another small step forward and she was delighted. I now had hope that the next goal - being able to stand - might be achievable as well.

Alison came back in on the Monday with the box. She had spent a considerable amount of time over the weekend setting up and testing the voicing tablet and it now worked perfectly. She asked me how I was as she approached the bed and I said, 'I am great' in my husky voice. I knew she would be pleased to hear me speak, but at the same time, she was deflated that the tablet would no longer be needed. I felt her mix of joy and disappointment but, at the end of the day, the power of speech was important to me and the voicing tablet would be available to other patients making their way along the rehabilitation journey.

During one of the subsequent days, one of the consultants suggested at a ward round that the ventilator was replaced with a 'circuit' and a floor-standing machine was brought in. It looked rather rudimentary when compared to the sophisticated machine that had been beside me and had helped me through such a bleak period in my life. I did not like the look of the machine and although logic told me that it was perfectly adequate and the team that had looked after me brilliantly were in no way going to put my welfare in any danger, I asked to be kept on the ventilator, for now, anyway. In time, the high-flow oxygen was replaced with a nasal cannula and my lungs had to work a little harder yet again. The tracheostomy remained in place to ensure I could cough and clear secretions from my lungs adequately, and I understood that it could be used for suction if there was any potential for further infection. Looking back, this was no problem although each big change was accompanied by considerable anxiety on my part, which was unnecessary as each adaptation went smoothly.

One morning, Sam, one of the facial deformity surgeons I work with and who is also a good friend, appeared in ICU. He had been messaging me and was keen to come and see me. He had finally managed to get past the nursing staff blocking him from visiting me in ICU. He had told them that he needed to check my tracheostomy as he is the hospital expert in this area. Sir Lancelot Spratt had returned. I imagined his car sitting outside with the door left open as he rushed in to see me. Somehow he had beaten the system, a challenge that he takes on regularly. He greeted me with his usual welcoming phrase, 'How are you, old boy?' It felt like old times and was reassuring. We had a lovely chat and he told me that the whole of the oral and maxillofacial surgery department had worried about me over the last two months and that whilst he could not pray for me as he is a furious atheist, he had, nevertheless, been thinking of me on a regular basis. It was great to see a familiar face in the environment that was now so familiar to me. He was the first mate I had held a conversation with in two months and we had a good moan about various topics in typical middle-aged male style! He then briefly looked at my tracheostomy site and was ejected by Sophie who wanted to do some physiotherapy stretches for me.

On day 82, Dr Shipley, one of the ICU consultants, came in casually dressed. It was a Saturday and he told me that the weather outside was fabulous. Dr Shipley had been out running and was full of the joys. He was like this most days and had a tremendous rapport with the nurses but for some reason, he was even more enthusiastic about life today. He was a lovely man and showed a great deal of empathy every time he came into ICU. I liked all seven of the ICU consultants. To me, they were now the 'Magnificent Seven'. Dr Shipley was quite laid back but I knew this was part of the act and, underneath, he was continually checking every detail and was not afraid to question anything that didn't seem right.

A chair was pulled up beside my bed and I was asked what I wanted to do that day. Immediately, my mind started racing and I thought about sitting at a terrasse in the south of France drinking a cold beer, or having lunch in a Spanish tapas bar. However, these were well out of reach so I had to moderate my thoughts somewhat. Before I said, 'Outside,' Dr Shipley was tapping something into his phone. He told me that the 'Magnificent Seven' sometimes seek additional advice from colleagues using a WhatsApp group and that he had just asked the others if there was any objection to the tracheostomy tube being removed. It came as a bit of a shock, but not altogether a surprise. I knew there would be no going back once it was out and that I would have to survive without it. After all, it had been doing nothing for several days and Dr Shipley had let me know that any plastic going through skin was an infection risk and might have been the reason for the most recent pseudomonas infection which had reappeared two days earlier. The decision had been made to treat this infection aggressively with nebulised antibiotics.

Dr Shipley gave the rest of the consultants two minutes to respond. There was only one response and that was in agreement. Within a matter of minutes, he had asked the nurses on duty to bring round a trolley and the equipment that was needed to remove the tracheostomy. The dressing and neck-strap were removed and the tracheostomy tube was removed. It only took a matter of seconds and fairly quickly a dressing was applied over the hole in my neck.

I was finally freed from the ventilator and whilst I was relieved to have respiratory independence, it was also scary. *What if I had a setback in my recovery and needed to go back to the ventilator?* Also, each time I coughed, the dressing 'blew' and air would come out of the hole and through the dressing. This was an unusual sensation but it was not painful in any way. I was glad to have been liberated from the tracheostomy and the neck-strap in particular.

Dr Shipley was persuasive with the nursing team and said to them that I no longer needed a doctor as a chaperone to go outside as I no longer needed a ventilator. Duly, a much reduced troupe accompanied me outside and Amanda was there to meet me as usual and we spent a seemingly long time chatting in the sunshine. As usual, there was the smoke curtain to go through and I was frustrated at the lack of consideration by the smokers in regard to the potential effect on a respiratory patient or non-smoker. On the way out, I asked the nurse pushing my wheelchair what the red heart was beside my bed. She told me that people had knitted red hearts and had given them to couples who had been separated by COVID-19, and as a result, Amanda and I had been given matching hearts. I shed a little tear thinking that a complete stranger had thought that our marriage would benefit from matching 'his' and 'her' hearts during our difficult period. Once outside, it felt exhilarating to finally be able to breathe in the fresh air without any mechanical respiration - true ventilation. I realised that I had not been weaned off the ventilator but in reality I had been weaned back on the natural ventilator, the air I love to breathe. Never had fresh air been so important to me.

CHAPTER 10

Rehabilitation of the Body, Mind and Spirit

IT WAS NOW the middle of June and although the critical illness was behind me, the light at the end of the tunnel was still dim. Robin had been moved to a respiratory ward and there was a big finale for the occasion. I was delighted for him and wished him well. I was now the only patient in ICU3. The routine of incarceration was reassuring but claustrophobic and I wanted some normality. Communication was now a two-way street. I could speak slightly more clearly and louder each day and could offer some conversation to the hospital staff. I could use my phone to text and use the internet even though my grip was poor and I still needed to use the table to wedge the phone to tap the keyboard.

As time went on, my energy increased and I would look forward to seeing the people who would come and go each day with a degree of regularity. Mornings were reserved for the drugs, breakfast, the ward round and physiotherapy. After lunch, I would sometimes have a little snooze. I like to have a little nap after lunch each day and during this phase of care, it was a little treat after a relatively strenuous morning. Sometimes the nursing staff turned the lights down for me too! The afternoons involved visits from the dietician, occupational therapy, speech and language therapy, a 'fun' physiotherapy activity and sometimes another snooze. I would then relax watching TV or a film on the tablet in time for dinner at 5pm. I would video call Amanda in the evenings which was a real tonic. It provided a bit of a finale to the day and I would be interested to hear what she had been doing; and I could now start to play a part in our marriage and provide some input to the decisions that needed to be made at home. I would then watch some more TV or another film. Staying awake until the 10pm drugs round worked well as this avoided a broken sleep overnight.

I could see a whiteboard on the wall opposite my bed and the nurses would write various things on it. It became a helpful piece of the environment. Sophie wrote on it one day: 'Daily Goal' and 'Weekly Goal'. We had a brief description and she encouraged me to vocalise these and have them written on the board. I had been doing goal-setting for around two weeks until this point but had not been sharing these with the team. Now was the time to make these 'public'. I had managed to relearn several routine tasks and I was relatively pleased with my progress. I could move my limbs and talk; the next goal was to stand. Further down the line, the goal was to walk but this would have to wait. Was being able to stand a weekly goal or would it take longer? It went on the board along with other weekly goals including trying to roll over in the bed overnight, reducing some of the medications (particularly the mirtazapine and the beta blocker) and the catheter removal. It was important to be able to stand not only by being upright, but also having fewer tubes and lines in my body and at the same time being able to remain upright with a relatively clearer head being less polluted with drugs. Subsequently, Niall, a nurse, structured the information on the whiteboard. He put the day and date at the top, the weather, sport, interests and goals towards the bottom and this remained for the rest of my time in ICU.

The word that made the most impact on conversation in ICU with me at this phase in my care was 'bees'. Everyone is fascinated by bees and I had wondered how my bees were doing. I hadn't been in the hive for some months and whilst I generally leave them alone over the winter, the spring is the busy time where the hive needs weekly attention to provide some additional feed (icing sugar and water), eliminate any emerging queens as two queens in a hive is a disaster and leads to a fight to the death, or worse still, half of the hive swarming with the existing queen to find a new place to live. This means a beekeeper will lose half of the bees, which leads to reduced honey production. It can be prevented by careful hive management. How I missed the routine of putting on my beekeeping suit, lighting the smoker and working through the frames in the hive. There were many conversations about the bees with a wide range of people and I would sometimes show people video recordings of the bees in my hive. It amazes the non-beekeeper just how the hive looks inside and works. It astonished me just what a conversation starter writing the word 'bees' on the board turned out to be. Coupled with this, Sherlock had been a hit with everyone on his visits outside so far and everyone with a dog wanted to know all about my faithful friend. Oh, how I missed him, but I enjoyed hearing all the dog lovers' stories about their dogs, particularly Vanessa, one of the nurses who treated her dogs like royalty. I thought her dogs keep her and her husband as pets, not the other way round.

The medical and nursing team continued to be very kind to me and looked after my every need. The nurses continued to talk continually to me and as my speech improved, I would try to hold other conversations with them. I became apprehensive about the practical side of life at home and at work and worried about how long I would be in hospital. The medical director of the hospital, Dr Johnstone, came to see me one day and put my mind at rest. I knew Dr Johnstone. She explained to me that I did not need to worry about my job as it would be held open for me since I had become infected at work. I was further relieved when she mentioned that I would be on full pay. The mortgage and the other bills would be paid, which was a relief.

One of the nurses casually asked me one day, 'What was it you used to do?' I am sure this was meant innocuously as she had no doubt come across many patients in ICU and coronary care who would never be able to go to back to work. I decided there and then that I would be going back to work. *But when?* was the question that ran through my mind. I reasoned that I was likely to be an in-patient for many months. It was not going to be my decision, but I reasoned that I would like to be out of hospital in six months and back at work in nine months. I would need to make a Herculean effort to meet these deadlines. The consultants told me to forget any notion of being back at work within 18 months and that I might not be able to do my job as was, and that there might need to be various workplace modifications if I had any level of disability. I appreciated this level of honesty but also the need to recover fully before being back at work. After all, I would not want to put my patients at risk because of my own health issues.

The mail porter would deliver the post to ICU3 and in amongst the post each day were various cards from family, friends and colleagues. I was just beginning to get my head round who was who, and what was what in the outside world, and was becoming familiar with current affairs and who was now missing from the news. I had realised that I was missing part of the year and wanted to know when exactly I fell ill so I could start to fill in more of the jigsaw. The staff told me that it was the end of May and that I had fallen ill at the end of March. I found a Wikipedia page listing the celebrities who had died, their date of death along with the cause of death. This was a boon and I could investigate one aspect of what I had missed. I was surprised that fewer important celebrities than I had expected had died. The list included Bill Withers, Honor Blackman, Little Richard, and I did shed a tear when I discovered that Nigel, the dog from *Gardeners' World*, had also been put to sleep. I was also confused by the continual mention of Dominic Cummings' eye test as well as other politicians that had tripped themselves up on the rules. These meant nothing to me until I did an internet trawl of recent current events. Sadly I later discovered that Annabelle, the mother of Amanda's closest friend, had also passed away, which saddened me.

I would ask the nurses to open each card and read it to me as I didn't have the coordination to be able to open envelopes and pull each card out. The nurses didn't know who the names were on each card but as I would smile, the nurses would ask how I knew each person and this helped me re-connect. One day, a large A4 envelope arrived and it was duly opened. It was a comb-bound book from my colleagues at the dental hospital and Zoe, my personal assistant, had collected a host of encouraging comments from my colleagues. One of the nurses started reading this and I was in tears. It was such a lovely gesture by everyone and I started to remember everyone I worked with. It went on the wall with many other cards and many people who came into ICU were intrigued by the book and wanted to read it. It was such a treat and I enjoyed having it read back time after time. I also started to respond to messages on my phone but I had to limit this to around one hour per day as I found my right shoulder would become very sore. The funny messages from friends would always be responded to, of course. One good friend of many years would start each message with 'Lazarus' and although he was being humorous, I knew there was an element of truth in his comment on my good fortune to be alive as well.

Later on in my ICU stay, I was put through a daily physical activity. I looked forward to these 11am sessions with excitement and trepidation in equal measure. On the first day, I sat on the edge of the bed with the help of Sophie, several physiotherapists and nurses. I felt so dizzy and was struggling to get enough oxygen into my lungs. I had been lying flat for nearly two months and sitting upright did not feel natural. I did my best to follow the reaching exercises with Sophie and her team. They were so enthusiastic and I knew that they had made this journey together as a team with many patients. This was reassuring. If other patients had made it successfully, there was no reason why I should not and could not do likewise. The reaching exercises involved stretching my arms out in front with the team supporting me and preventing me from falling over. My back was agony and could not hold me up so I needed a nurse to support me from behind with a pillow. I was pleased to complete the exercises, albeit simple ones, but I felt terrible and I was so glad to lie back in bed. I was totally exhausted as well. *Why had such a simple task taken so much out of me? Would I ever be able to lead a normal life again or was this it?*

Gradually more strenuous workouts were put in place for my limbs which were very weak due to extensive muscle wasting (atrophy). By this point I had lost 26kg – estimated to be 75% of skeletal muscle loss. The next task was to go on the Tilt Table. I was rolled onto the transfer sheet and slid across onto the Tilt Table as the next stage of the process towards standing and eventually walking. It was not pleasant but it was not my place to complain. After all, the team were doing their best for me. The movement on the Tilt Table started. My head was gradually elevated and my feet lowered. My body went haywire. My breathing went out of control, my heart raced, my blood pressure went through the roof and I felt awful. In my head, this was a torture table, a medieval rack similar to the ducking stool. I quietly questioned the purpose of the torture table as it was so unpleasant. I was moved back into bed and as I lay exhausted, I wondered what other machines the team had access to in order to help my physical recovery. *Would these break my spirit or would I conquer these mentally first and then succeed physically?*

The next day, I was given a break from the Tilt Table; another machine came in its place. This was a Stand Aid but there was no chance of me standing at this point. Again, I was shuffled to sit on the edge of the bed with the help of Sophie, the physiotherapy team and nurses, and the machine was moved towards my weak shins. I could feel my razor-sharp shins touch the pads on the machine. I was to lean forward and put some weight through my legs and feet. How dreadful I felt along with wicked dizziness and feeling sick. It was not good but I persisted with massive encouragement from the team and was glad to lie back in bed shortly after. It was a Friday and as the weekend beckoned for the physiotherapy team, I bade them farewell. I recognised that the team deserved some much needed time off.

Over the weekend, the on-call physiotherapist, Steven, came to see me. I hadn't met him before but I knew he would be a good man from the initial conversation we had. Steven undertook muscle and joint stretches on the Saturday and certainly put me through my 'paces'. After he left, I felt drained. I had not been to the gym since being a student but I had enjoyed the session with him. Did I sleep well that afternoon or what? I was stiff on the Sunday and one of the other physiotherapists did some more gentle work with me. I was relieved but knew that this was going to be the only day of rest this week. Monday came and the Tilt Table was again wheeled towards my bed. I had the feeling of dread wash over me but what was I to do? I would much prefer to conquer the predicament I was in. Again I was rolled onto the transfer mat and slid across. As with the previous occasion, the straps were fastened around my feet, waist and chest to stop me from falling out. I was tilted from horizontal to around 60 degrees and I could feel my body weight pushing hard through my hips, knees and ankles. Even though I had lost so much weight, I had not had any substantial weight through my major joints for weeks and they were not in good condition. Sophie wanted me to get my arms moving as well and asked me to 'pretend punch' Katie, one of the other physiotherapists. I managed to punch five times with each hand even though it was a struggle. I hadn't worked out, until this point that Sophie does not negotiate. I stupidly suggested I could do another five punches with each hand and everyone watched as Sophie held me to my word. I was totally destroyed and felt shattered. I knew not to try to beat Sophie in the future.

The dizziness the Tilt Table caused on this day was ghastly and I needed peace and quiet to recover. The problem was that I couldn't breathe and felt very unwell. I was hyperventilating yet my oxygen saturation was dropping. My heart was racing (tachycardia) and my blood pressure was raised. I had pain across my chest and in my left shoulder. I couldn't work out if the pain was from the physiotherapy work over the weekend or if it was something else. My training had taught me that pain anywhere from the face down to the hand on the left side could be a heart attack. *Oh no, was I deteriorating again?* The ECG physiologist was called urgently. Everyone was hanging around at the end of the ward discussing the events. I was worried less by the pain and other symptoms but more by the fact that everyone else was so concerned. The physiologist came quickly. I was used to being hooked up to a 3-lead ECG. Whenever the machine would sound a fault, I got to know that it would be the green lead, and the nurses would know the green lead was the issue. This time, 10 leads were attached to my chest and after a few minutes, the tracing was checked by one of the consultants, Dr Morris.

Fortunately, it was normal. I had not suffered a heart attack or any other heart rhythm problem. However, there was no answer for my symptoms. I was feeling no better and asked Dr Morris if I could start a beta-blocker to help with anxiety and regularise my heartbeat which was concerning me. She agreed and I was started on the beta-blocker and another medicine to deal with anxiety. I asked the nursing staff if I could go to sleep and the lights were duly dimmed. I slept for hours, through lunch and well into the afternoon. I felt much better when I awoke and my now cold lunch was still sitting on the tray. Everyone was content that I seemed to feel better. The nurses were extremely kind and left me to myself for the rest of the afternoon. It was a quiet evening before a long night's sleep.

The physiotherapists continued with the joint and muscle work each day, increasing my core flexibility and strength with a view to my standing. This would be done with exercises either sitting on the edge of the bed or using the Stand Aid machine. When sitting on the edge of the bed, I would be asked to stretch out with each hand, lean over to touch the opposite knee and to run my hands down my legs. Initially this was almost impossible and having lain horizontally for over two months, the feeling of being upright was horrible. It was made worse by these exercises but I knew they were the route to success so persevered on every occasion. It was sore to contort my body into different positions and I needed much encouragement. They were brilliant and although they would give me the option of stopping, this is not in my nature and I wanted to get better so made sure I did exactly what was requested. The exercises punctuated my day and each little metaphorical step forward was important in the journey back to health, however small and seemingly insignificant. I hungered to be back to my old self and wanted to be able to do the things I enjoyed, such as going for walks with Sherlock Bones, golf, skiing and motorcycling.

The Stand Aid machine had a large belt that would be placed round my back and it would be tightened to pull me into the machine. I would lean forwards onto the armrests. With a physiotherapist in control, the motor would move the armrests and belt vertically and after many days practising, I was able to stand on day 81. That my first stand in three months was extremely short was irrelevant, I had finally been able to stand even though it was painful due to my weak legs. I sat back on the bed. What an achievement and everyone around seemed more delighted than me. Perhaps I was making progress after all. Later that day it felt like a major achievement and I video called Amanda that evening to share my joy with her. I slept soundly that night dreaming of walking again one day. These video calls became very important to me and broke up the evenings. They seemed to coincide with the nurses' break and so they were happy to set up the tablet for me and, as time went on, leave me to make the call myself. Amanda was fantastic and was only unavailable in the evenings on a few occasions. Although I appreciated she also had her own life to live, it was hard not to have the opportunity to speak to her on these occasions. I also video called Callum and Colin on a few occasions. I did not feel that I had enough energy to call other family and friends for fear of disappointing them in being unable to hold a coherent conversation.

Gary, one of my favourite nurses was a tremendous help when I wanted to video call my mum. Aged 89 and with vascular dementia meaning she can be confused and forgetful, my family had protected her from the bad news and their helplessness at the situation over the previous two months. At this point, she was only partially apprised of my situation. I wanted to make contact with her. I had by this point missed Mothers' Day, Easter and her birthday and I felt guilty. Amanda and Callum had, of course, taken care of all three events but I was oblivious at this point. Callum duly arranged to go to her house and help her get online and Gary, knowing that I would be very emotional, ran a masterclass in being the master of ceremonies. He made sure everyone was comfortable speaking over the video call, made sure everyone could hear and see properly and 'chipped in' little pieces of information to help me with what was a difficult conversation. He was a marvel and I was grateful for this help along with so many other delightful encounters over the weeks I spent in ICU3. Gary was an excellent nurse on every occasion. More reassuringly, as I write, I can reflect that there are still real gentlemen in this world.

My first cousin, once removed, George, kept in the background and knew that the boundary between family and doctor should be kept thus. He would come to see me with another doctor who would take the lead on my care. George was, nevertheless, keen to ensure I was as happy as possible and I asked him for a favour. He had played the violin at his father's funeral two weeks before I fell ill and I recall being moved by the occasion. I asked George if he would play for me in ICU. He was given approval to do this by the consultants and duly brought his violin in. It was not any old violin, it originally belonged to his great-grandmother who

'DYING TO LIVE'

was my grandmother and I remember it being played when I was a small child. George duly satisfied my request and it was thrilling to listen to a virtuoso violin concert in ICU. I would imagine that was a first for all the staff as well as me - what a treat. I am sure George's father, my cousin who was also a doctor, would have been very proud.

CHAPTER 11

Last Man Standing

AS THE DAYS went on, I became tired of the liquid tomato feed that gradually dripped into my stomach through the nasogastric tube. I was not hungry but knew that I was a shadow of my former self. Arianne, the dietician, came to see me again and suggested I try some soft and almost runny food not only to start eating something different but to re-start my digestive system with different textures of food. It would take time for my gut to start working properly and this was yet another part of my body that had been on strike for several weeks. I wondered what soft food would taste like. I had no appetite and my senses of smell and taste were non-functional. Everything smelled of nothing if that makes sense. Arianne explained that it would be important to push through this barrier, however difficult. I decided that fruit jelly and custard would be the place to start. I hadn't eaten anything for over two months so was not in a place to start with the Sunday roast.

That day I texted Amanda to ask if some jelly and custard pots could be delivered to the hospital for me. Anna's partner, Lawrence, was asked to do the hospital drop-off. He is a police officer in the city and as he was on his way to work he came into the hospital in uniform. I was told that the police had turned up to see me. The police regularly interview patients suspected of being involved in crimes or who had been victims of crimes but as I was not the type to associate with the criminal world, Lawrence was turned swiftly away despite his protestations. I quickly worked out what was going on and texted the family to ask Lawrence if he could come back later. He duly managed to return later in the day and all was sorted.

I couldn't open the lid of the jelly pot as my grip was so poor. Martyn, one of the nurses, stepped in and spooned little pieces of jelly into my mouth. Swallowing was still painful due to the nasogastric tube but I persevered. It was strange to start eating again and I felt that I was a small child being weaned. I didn't realise it at the time but this was not far from the truth.

The nasogastric tube suddenly became blocked. The nurse who was in charge that day was used to unblocking these. She tried everything including the physical, the mechanical, syringing fluids into it and applying suction. After half an hour it became obvious that it was futile. I hated it so much that I asked her just to remove it and she said to Arianne later that there was no option. Arianne was firm with me and let me know that it would need to be replaced unless I started eating 3,000 calories per day. I did not want it replaced so I was determined to eat anything that came my way from then on. I started to eat solid food for the first time in two and a half months. There was a pattern to my meals, with porridge at breakfast, a main meal at lunchtime and finger food in the evening. The lunchtime meals were substantial and I did my best to eat everything. I ate my way through this hurdle and was allowed some flexibility with the evening meal as time went on. The executive chef in the main kitchen would cook almost whatever was asked. It nearly became a game to see if I could defeat chef!

I had no idea about the role of an occupational therapist until this point in my journey. Cerys and Janine came as a double act to ICU3 on most afternoons to mobilise my arms, ensure the movement of my wrists and fingers was normal and determine if there would be any aids that would help with getting me more independent when drinking, eating, texting and so on. They would spend around an hour with me every afternoon and as the weeks unfolded, I got to know them well. They also got to know me well and, like the physiotherapists, had made this critical care journey with other patients before. They, too, had been with me from the beginning of the ICU journey and did everything they could to help me. There were standard tests to assess my hand function. The nine-hole peg test and the dynamometer to test my grip strength became regulars. It is safe to say that I didn't get the best of results the first time these were used. I did at least complete them both. It was not a success but at least it was not failure either.

Cerys and Janine were interested in my job as an orthodontist and whilst they made no guarantee that I would return to work, they encouraged me to set this as a long-term goal, accepting that some adaptations might be needed if I had any issues with mobility or function. Dr Morris, one of the consultants, brought me Play-Doh and a game of draughts to help me with my hand function. Moulding the Play-Doh in my hands was very therapeutic and helped me start using both hands together. I also played draughts with the nurses, and although a simple task, lifting the counters was exceptionally difficult at the beginning, but it was good at getting my fingers working. Cerys and Janine brought in Connect Four occasionally and although it was a children's game, I got the idea that it was to help my hands and arms start moving, but it was tiring.

One of the consultants, Dr McCloud, was in ICU3 one afternoon when the OTs were working with me. Sophie happened to be around at the same time. I had been asked if there was anything that could help me and I jokingly said that I would love a gin and tonic. Quick as a flash, he suggested that alcohol could be prescribed for seriously or terminally ill patients and that this was appropriate for me. It was felt that a gin and tonic might be good for my arms as I would have to lift the cup myself rather than using a straw as I had been doing until this point. A two-handled cup with a lid containing a one-way valve was found and given to me. I duly regaled the tale to Amanda that evening and asked if she could bring in a bottle of gin and a bottle of tonic, which she did the next day. Less excitingly, the OTs brought me a plate guard to fit around the dinner plate so that I could load my fork with a foam handle and be less messy when feeding myself. It became a bit of a chimps' tea party though.

I was determined to start flossing my teeth again and with a great deal of time and effort I eventually managed to floss my lower incisors. This was yet another goal achieved and I added another tooth further back in my mouth into the regime periodically as my hands improved, little by little.

Each time I looked ahead, I could see the wheelchair in clear view. I had no complaint about its location, nonetheless, I wondered constantly if I would be disabled for the rest of my life. *Was this going to be my new norm?* Sophie and her team were very clever at encouraging me to look to the long-term and have a clear expectation of what I would want to achieve physically, accepting that my body might not fully recover. There were so many variables: the unknown impact of COVID-19, the probability that my lungs were severely damaged and might not recover adequately and the amount of effort I was prepared to invest in my recovery. It became clear to me that I was recovering from parallel conditions: COVID-19 and the critical illness journey. The staff had lots of information about recovering from critical illness but little to go on in relation to COVID-19. I was shocked when one of the consultants shared an ICU secret with me that so much of medicine is trial and error. It was worrying but true. At no point did they put my life in any danger, but each minor change was monitored carefully with the effect being noted and assessed, then re-assessed. Anything untoward was discussed among the team and a solution would be found. I thought about my specialty of orthodontics and treatment for facial deformity and realised I am professionally risk adverse and have the luxury to offer patients treatment options that have lots of history and evidence to support them, but as a specialty, we tend to treat patients to textbook normals rather than addressing their main concern and leaving things at that. It made me think long and hard about orthodontic 'treatment' or orthodontic 'care'. *Which is correct?*

Visits outside to meet Amanda continued and I became well enough to be hoisted into the wheelchair and gradually the amount of equipment and number of staff required for each trip reduced. On one occasion we went outside and as it was so sunny Dr McJoss treated Amanda and me to an ice cream. This was a massive treat. I was spoiled in the last week of my stay in ICU3 in other ways.

I started to realise that my other body senses were not working properly. Sophie would ask me to close my eyes and touch my chin, my nose and my forehead every day she came to see me. I knew from my days studying basic sciences at university that Sophie was testing my sense of body awareness (proprioception) and although I nearly poked an eye out the first time I tried to touch my nose and could not reach my forehead, with practice over several weeks, I eventually conquered this. Looking back, my proprioception sense being non-functional was probably why I could not feel my arms or legs when I first awoke. My other senses were also 'out of kilter'. Lack of balance (equilibrioception) and dizziness were dreadful and required anti-sickness medication. Although my body ached, I could not feel external pain. I have tickly feet and our cat Smudge Tuxedo (a black and white flighty cat) exploits this at night by terrorising my toes and the soles of my feet if they are outside the duvet. Amanda also tortures my toes as she walks past if they dare to be exposed. The junior doctors would run an instrument along the soles of my feet at every ward round to test my reflexes and the perception of pain (nociception). For the first time in my life, I would not instantaneously jump and lift my knees to my chest when anyone came within the ten feet exclusion zone of my feet! If only Smudge had been there, I would finally have been able to win a small battle.

I wondered how Smudge was doing as well as Sherlock Bones, our fish, chickens and bees. Smudge is Amanda's cat. Whilst he weaves in and out of my legs when I feed him and he comes begging with eyes the size of a planet when I am eating tuna, battered fish and indeed chips, I am convinced that the rest of the time he is plotting to kill me so that he can be one step closer to his mama, Amanda. Why does he insist on sitting like the Lion King at the top of the stairs making me attempt to leap two stairs and unceremoniously slip, trip and drop whatever I am carrying, only to jump onto his pedestal and wag the tip of his tail? If my arm is hanging over the arm of a chair, why is it his right to attack my fingers like a leopard killing a gazelle only to devour it later? He has even been known to creep round the arm of the couch and attack me from behind my head in the same way a tiger would prey on a water buffalo in the mangrove.

Smudge, like many cats, had a brush with death as a kitten and lost one of his nine lives. He ran out from the house in front of a car and escaped with a broken leg. He limped back home, bedraggled. It cost £2,000 for the orthopaedic vet to fit an external fixator to allow the broken bones to heal. We had an interesting six-week period where we had to cage him to prevent him climbing the radiators, curtains and blinds as the wirework of the fixator would get caught and we would have to disentangle a hanging cat. When caged, he would get entangled in the wirework and dealing with an angry, caged and entangled cat is no mean feat. Although Smudge Tuxedo is the silent assassin in our house, I have managed to survive many patricide attempts on my life and I missed him, even though he tests my nociception sense in his own special way.

Finally, I could not feel heat through my skin and I now know that my sense of heat (thermoception) was non-functional for the first few weeks of recovery. How unusual. I had previously loved to sit in front of our log fire and enjoy the heat as it roared away like a wild beast, spitting occasionally like a tormented snake and pumping out pulses of heat to warm the room and most of the house. I could feel cold but not heat and, surprisingly, I did not sweat even weeks down the line on the ward when the other patients were lying in bed half naked with the summer sun streaming through the windows. Sweating is a rather personal subject, but its purpose is to evaporate, cooling the body. Although I put in a lot of energy in the gym and worked hard physically as a ward patient, I didn't seem to ever get warm or overheat. I realised that the effect of critical illness from COVID and being asleep for so long had upset all of my senses and although hearing, sight, touch, smell, taste, proprioception, pain, balance and thermoception had returned in this order, it was all rather strange. I had, of course, come to my senses, even though my family have been asking me to do this for years!

One of the nurses, Katy, of whom I became fond, had suffered a difficult break-up with her long-term boyfriend and had thrown herself into her work. She came in bouncing one Saturday and announced that today would be my 'spa' day. It was the first time I had had my hair washed in many weeks and although it was done with a bucket underneath the end of the bed, it felt good to be clean up top. The standard bedbath ritual was undertaken with the usual tenderness and attention to detail, with various fragrances and lotions applied. Katy massaged my legs and feet, trimmed all my nails and tidied up my beard. The latter had been avoided until this point as I had a bizarre notion that any trimmings might end up in the tracheostomy hole. The catheter was removed the next day. I now could use a bottle and urinate as needed. I worried about wetting the bed but this turned out to be an unnecessary concern, all went fine and it was a little bit more independence and another step closer to normality. A few days later, I felt well enough to even have a bath. The nurses explored all options within nearby wards. Some were closed due to COVID-19 and others had been requisitioned but an available bath was found elsewhere in the hospital and I was hoisted into the wheelchair one evening, whisked round to the ward and had a bath, albeit less leisurely than I would normally enjoy since I don't customarily bathe with the assistance of several nurses. It was great to sleep that night having had a good soak. I was starting to feel more human.

Having had some fairly wild thoughts and dreams in the weeks since waking up, I knew that my mental health had improved. However, I had no idea of what was to come so I asked the consultants to make contact with Scott, a clinical psychologist who I knew a little. He came the next day. He also returned a week later to do a follow-up session and we hatched a plan to help me with the rest of my journey. The major worry was that I would end up with post-traumatic stress disorder down the line but at least I knew the warning signs. I also asked to see one of the hospital chaplains, an exceptional lady who helped me get so much of what had happened earlier in the journey into perspective. We also shared a prayer for those who had looked after me, supported both me and our family, and of course for those families who had not been as fortunate.

I would watch films and TV shows on the hospital tablet enjoying the familiarity of some that I had watched many times over. There was something reassuring about these. Monty Python's *Meaning of Life* was watched over and over again, and fortunately by now, the python that I thought was trying to kill me from the ceiling has been dealt with. I was able to breathe without worry. *Top Gun*, my favourite film was also watched a few times. Sadly, one day the tablet which had been propped up on the over-the-bed table slid off while the table was being moved and smashed on the floor. That was the end of the tablet and I had to make do with watching TV on my phone.

I was keeping up to date with the news and accessing this on my phone daily, but was struck dumb by the reports of people, without good reason, not wearing a mask in public with these selfish individuals somehow seeming to think that they have no responsibility for the health of the rest of the population. Music continued to be a constant pleasure throughout the ICU period and helped me relax in the evenings prior to sleeping. Andrea was, and still is, a regular favourite along with some regular and more eclectic rock, pop and classical music.

I started to read books again. It had taken some time to have the concentration to be able to read and follow a story. Reading news websites and internet in general had helped train my brain in readiness. I also wanted to use my work laptop, but just couldn't remember the username/password combination. A colleague had sent me some books through the internal mail on subjects I enjoy. I particularly like the *Para Handy* books featuring a hapless boat captain who would sail his steamboat, the *Vital Spark*, up and down the west coast of Scotland always ending in disaster - a bit like a Scottish version of *Only Fools and Horses*. It offered an insight into life in the west of Scotland in a bygone era when my parents were children. Many of the stories resonated with me. I also read one of Terry Waite's books. He was an envoy for the Church of England and had tried to seek the release of four hostages in Lebanon having previously negotiated the release of many others, but was tricked and was himself kept as a hostage for nearly five years. His book, *Taken on Trust,* was of considerable interest to me as although I was not held captive by terrorists or indeed for anything like the same length of time, the solutions he found to help deal with captivity became very useful for me. I found the strategy of tracing familiar pleasant journeys from childhood through to my present life helped with boredom and difficulty in sleeping. Learning to live in the moment, however, and not being frustrated with the past, and not wallowing in self-pity were more difficult.

The difference between Terry Waite and me was, as the nurse said, 'being safe'. Having been held as a hostage must have been a much more difficult situation. How Terry Waite coped with this I do not know and I reasoned with myself that I was far more

'DYING TO LIVE'

fortunate. I read and re-read the same line in the book time and time again. 'What I need to do is accept the moment for what it is.' This sentence hit home each time I read it. There would be no point in trying to read too much into having been struck down with the horrible COVID-19 disease. An acceptance of the situation was one crucial step in the recovery journey. I was, after all alive and the medical problems that had beset the ECMO stage were now long behind me and I was recovering. Logic dictated that practical planning for each situation as it arose would be best. To strategise and solutionise would be futile. Many potential scenarios might not ever occur. Becoming medically healthy was important now (stage 2), following survival (stage 1) and then the physical rehabilitation could be intensified to make me independent again to be able to go home (stage 3), before the final, but much longer phase of home-based rehabilitation (phase 4) to reach a level of fitness and stamina that would allow me to function normally. By now, I had decided that I wanted to return to work within nine months of falling ill and be back at full strength in one year with golf having started by Christmas, skiing by Easter and motorcycling by the summer. The doctors and rehabilitation team thought these goals were all unlikely, especially being back at work in a relatively short space of time.

As the weeks rolled on, the nurses started to provide less help for me and this was necessary to reduce my dependence on them. I had enjoyed the pampering and almost continual assistance for every task but I realised the change was preparing me for moving to a general ward. What the nurses reduced in terms of help, they replaced with fun. Dr Morris had earlier brought in a game of draughts for me and I continued to play several of the nurses and, without bragging, I won on more than one occasion. It helped me with handling the counters and the OTs brought smaller and smaller versions of Connect Four, which required increasing levels of manual dexterity. Cards appeared and one evening there was a competition game of the TV programme *The Chase*. I was the loser, but one of the nurses had brought in chocolate bars as prizes for everyone. What fun. There was also a casino game but I will refrain from mentioning any more here as nurses would never gamble with a patient...

As discharge day from ICU approached, the medical step-down continued. I was apprehensive about the speed of this and wanted to stay in ICU longer as it was a cosseted environment and I felt I was making good progress. I worried that the pace would be jeopardised on a ward. All the lines in my arms were removed over a few days. There was a spectacular fountain of blood from my left wrist when Trish, one of the nurses, removed the arterial line. It went everywhere but I couldn't do anything to help. Pressure was applied with a gauze swab. Each time the pressure was removed, I was fascinated by the blood pulsing into the air. It was quite a bloodbath and it took some time to get it under control. I reasoned with myself that having had so many trans-fusions that it wasn't my blood! The bed needed changed, and luckily, for once, it was not due to a toilet accident. I was finally free of pipes and lines going into or exiting my body, except for the nasal cannula and oxygen therapy. The support boots were no longer needed and I could move my arms and legs in the bed without something tugging or getting tangled. I was free and ready for the next stage of rehabilitation.

On day 86 it was ICU discharge day. It was a day that we had been working towards for some time. I awoke to some very cheery nurses. It was a strange day for them too and felt a bit like the end of an important part of the COVID-19 story for them as well as me. After all, ICU3 was going to return to be the day surgery recovery suite and many of the team had been redeployed from other areas of the hospital. They were now going back to their original jobs and would be back working with colleagues they had missed. There was a sense of energy about the day as it unfolded. Tracey, one of the charge nurses, came in with an extra spring in her step. Her husband is a chef and she had, along with him, prepared a special breakfast for me. I enjoyed a lovely bowl of muesli and yoghurt and then some soft fruit. Her husband had baked me some croissants and pains au chocolat. I was full after the muesli, yoghurt and fruit and simply couldn't eat the bread products, but it was such a lovely treat.

And what a morning! Doctors and nurses came to see me in ICU to wish me well and to say goodbye to the nurses who were moving back to their base. It was a happy day for everyone. Looking back, there was a degree of elation that this might be the end of the first wave of the pandemic for the hospital. I was given a bedbath as normal and the hospital communications team came to see me for a press release. Amanda and Callum had supplied a form of words as well to accompany my statement. There was not to be any in-depth physiotherapy on this day, the energy required would be needed to transition to a ward.

I transferred to a wheelchair with the help of the Stand Aid machine with minimal help from the physiotherapists and took a few minutes to compose myself. It was time to leave the bed and the ward that had become my own, literally. The communications team captured the journey out of ICU and along the corridors to the respiratory ward. Little did I know how many people had turned up to line the corridor outside ICU3 to clap me as I was pushed along the corridor. The medical staff, nursing staff and allied health professionals who had been caring for me were there in force clapping. A number of the staff that I had redeployed from the Dental Hospital to Ninewells were there along with my good friends Sam and Kunal. As ever Kunal loves a bit of razzmatazz and had some pots and pans to make some noise. He high-fived me as I went past and I later found out that he had got into trouble for breaking the social distancing rules, which meant nothing to me at that point. In fact, none of the new social norms that had emerged in the preceding three months meant anything to me. I had been locked-up while the country was locked down.

I had won the second battle and was medically healthy. It was a joyous occasion for the ICU staff who had collectively steered me through the most difficult patch in my life. I appreciated that it was also a big win for them as they had had a dreadful time during the first wave and now felt they understood the major aspects of COVID-19 disease and how serious it could be. They were now better prepared, but apprehensive about the second wave, expected in the autumn. The Operational Leadership Team meeting in the hospital had asked for frequent updates on my condition and one of my managerial colleagues told me that everyone at the meeting on my discharge from ICU was somewhat relieved that I had got to this point. Even the chief executive commented that he was pleased to see such a positive outcome.

My survival story seemed to be of interest. The hospital posted the video of me being wheeled through the hospital on their Facebook page later in the day and it attracted 1.1 million views with thousands of comments from family, friends, colleagues and well-wishers.

I was titled the 'sickest survivor' and, to this day, I am told that few patients have survived the level of critical illness that I endured. I wanted the story to give hope to those with relatives suffering from COVID-19 and to alert the population to how serious the infection can be, but more importantly to encourage the population to avoid catching it in the first place. The accompanying newspaper article was reproduced across eight newspapers the next day. My mother was delighted that I even had greater coverage than the Scottish First Minister that day. One of the newspapers even used the title, 'Last Man Standing Leaves ICU'.

CHAPTER 12

Eat, Sleep, Rehab and Repeat

I WAS APPREHENSIVE about moving to a general respiratory ward but knew it was a step closer to getting home. Moving to this ward was like moving house with all the stuff that was brought round with me. I hadn't realised just how much I had accumulated in the three months I had been in hospital. There were two trolleys full of personal items and my brown bag of clothes. I was given a bed in Bay 1, near the nurses' station so that they could keep an eye on me. I was hoisted from the wheelchair to the bed and had a huge sigh of relief once the oxygen was plugged into the supply on the wall. One of the nurses checked my observations and all was in order. I was pleased that my oxygen level was an acceptable 92%. My blood pressure and pulse were relatively normal. I would be okay. It had been a big day and I was out of energy. I was no celebrity there, just another patient along with five other ill men and women. Luckily I was next to an old friend from ICU3, Robin. He looked over and welcomed me. It was nice to see a familiar face.

The nurses welcomed me to the ward and during their handover, all the drugs I was taking, and my various needs such as a bottle/bedpan for toileting and the rehabilitation plans were discussed. Every aspect of my care was covered. I had been using a fabulous bed in ICU which had an air mattress and was fully electric. The bed I was given on the ward wasn't so good for me at this point in my recovery though. I am no wimp and like a relatively hard bed to sleep on but this was unbearable as I was so thin and had so little muscle and no fat to give me any cushioning. A bed with an air mattress was found in a relatively short space of time and I was transferred with the glide sheet since I was so tired. This was much better. I ate a small lunch and fell asleep. Deborah, one of the ICU liaison nurses came to see me in the afternoon to make sure everything was okay and I was happy to let her know that I was being well looked after. Sophie came to see me as well to check that there was nothing that needed to be sorted. She was a constant throughout the journey and was amazing at looking after every need I had. I was given an afternoon off from physiotherapy but the work was to re-start the following day.

The ward was noisy. I had been on my own in ICU3 for some time and I needed to get used to the hustle and bustle of a general ward. Worse still, I had to get used to the fact that I was now one of six patients being looked after by one nurse, not the other way round. No longer would there be time for the nurses to help me with food, take time to chat to me, watch the TV with me, play games or attend to my little whims. I was now going to have to be more independent and take my turn in the queue. It was an interesting first night. I video called Amanda as usual and the background noise meant I had to turn up the volume to hear her. Edith, diagonally opposite me was troubled. She would wander up and down the ward, getting in and out of bed and argue with the nurses. Night seemed to blend with the day for her and the nurses would have to escort her back to bed every time and try to settle her. Billy opposite me snored like a train. I snore too, in fact everyone does, even our dog Sherlock. But this was impressive. He would gasp for air and let out the most enormous long snore with his lips vibrating like a child blowing a raspberry. There was a young guy next to me. He had his headphones on constantly, presumably watching TV or films. Luckily he wasn't noisy but he did have his bed lamp on until the small hours of the night. *How would I sleep with all this going on?* And the noise elsewhere in the ward was spectacular, it felt like I was trying to sleep in a train station. Patients were brought in during the night to empty beds, some patients would shout out in their sleep and the clatter of things being cleaned or dropped continued throughout the night. Then the curtains were opened and it was the next day. I was exhausted and wondered how I would cope with this on an ongoing basis.

The nurses also worked 12-hour shifts in this ward. I later discovered that this system had been introduced at the beginning of the COVID-19 season and, as the nurses preferred this, it was to stay. The nursing handover again took place at 7:40 but with six patients in each bay, it took much longer than I had known from before. Medicines were dispensed at 8:00 and I thought it must be a challenge to get the medicines exactly right for every patient, every time. I had been weaned off a number of the tablets and capsules in ICU so the medicine rounds were now much simpler for me. I would duly take the tablets and capsules quickly with some water. There was also the twice daily nebuliser to kill off the remaining pseudomonas infection in my lungs.

Although it sounded like Darth Vader in a phone box, I did not want pseudomonas to return at any cost and knew that it had plagued Annabelle, the mother of our dear friend, for years and she had never been able to shift it fully. She had been in this ward many times and I had come to visit her. Her death had been the low point of the year for her family and I knew I had to overcome pseudomonas. I did not want to become a long-term respiratory patient. The nebuliser required to be put together on each occasion, the powder mixed with saline, left to dissolve and then be poured into the reservoir before being inhaled over a period of ten minutes or so. I learned not to joke about it being a 'bong' as some of the patients around me were recovering drug addicts. It was good to get this out of the way before breakfast when the morning routine allowed. Breakfast was just porridge but Liz, a super nurse, made me a cup of tea, and it was in a china cup. What a treat.

It was Friday and the ward round was next. The ward round had fewer doctors than the equivalent in ICU, and I noticed that, because there were many more patients to see in the ward, the doctors worked in teams and the patients who needed less medical input would be seen relatively quickly by the junior team. Those who had just been admitted or were in greater medical need were seen by the consultant and their team first. I could overhear the classic question to some confused patients, 'Who is the Prime Minister?' At least now I knew the answer without difficulty although I felt for those who struggled with the question each time. The consultant on duty today was Dr Long. He was brilliant and came to see Robin first. The curtain was pulled round but I overheard the conversation that he was only likely to be in hospital for another week. How nice I thought for Robin to be able to get home to his family. I wondered when I might get home, but quickly realised that I had a lot ahead of me as I couldn't even stand properly or walk.

Dr Long and the team then came to me. He smiled and welcomed me to the ward. He knew my story well and asked if there was anything he could do to make my stay as comfortable as possible. I knew he couldn't do much about the noise overnight and that I just had to accept this. I would adjust to the greater number of people, the noise and the fact I was now a small fish in a bigger pond. I had dealt with this many times in life, as one of three brothers, as one boy in amongst many Scouts, at school, university and life to date. I said to him that I would be fine after I adjusted to the new environment. He laughed and said that I would have my eyes opened. I wondered what he meant. My drug chart was checked along with my observation chart. The oxygen levels were satisfactory along with the other vital signs. Dr Long and his team were happy and mentioned that the next period of recovery was all about rehabilitation and seeing how far oxygen support could be reduced. It would be a slog and I would need to work hard. Results would be directly proportional to effort. I understood this logic and had by now got used to the fact that this was a mental battle as well as a physical journey.

The rehabilitation schedule now moved up a gear. It was all about the goal of standing and becoming independent. The initial plan was to consolidate standing. As I could now transfer from bed to wheelchair without the need to be hoisted, it was so much easier to get back and forth. I now used the Stand Aid to help me get vertical but not needing the crane was a big bonus, not only for me, but for everyone. We practised this extensively using the Stand Aid machine by transferring from bed to wheelchair and back to bed again. Now Sophie or one of her incredible staff would do some joint stretches and joint mobility work at 9am with me for around 30 minutes or so while the ward round was going on. Depending on their workload, they would then come back later on in the morning at around 11am for another short session. I still required a bedbath and had to fit in with the washing needs of the other patients in the bay. The familiarity of this pattern was reassuring.

Cerys and Janine would come at around 11.30am for my occupational therapy session. Lunch came at exactly 12.30pm and was usually a decent meal. Once lunch had been cleared away, I would regularly have a pleasant little snooze. The afternoon was dedicated to rest and physiotherapy with food again at 5pm, and then a quiet evening before the lights went out around 10pm. Even though my body ached, I realised that the 'no pain equals no gain' mantra held true and I would need to push on, irrespective of any discomfort. My appetite for rehabilitation as well as food was by now increasing and I knew that I had to rebuild my body having lost 26kg at the worst point. It was a case of eat, sleep, rehab and repeat.

Arianne, the dietician, kept in touch with me while on the ward and would check what I was eating along with my weight every week. She wanted to check that I was eating 3,000 calories per day. I hadn't been able to do this in ICU, and since leaving, I was not gaining weight. It was time to change the strategy. The hospital menu was reasonable but was not providing me with the calories I needed, even with the daily high-calorie milkshake and the high protein drinks that I had been taking for many weeks. The latter were disgusting and rather than diluting the little sachets, I preferred to take the sachet neat. It felt like a shot of some yucky spirit on a boys' night out, except that there was no night out. There was a conversation at the start of the ward round the following day about what to do. Arianne suggested to Dr McDonald, the consultant on duty that day that she could ask Amanda to bring in food from home. The senior charge nurse was called and mentioned that the health and safety rules precluded heating up patient's food. Dr McDonald was not impressed and told her that this was to be ignored and if I needed food from home then the nursing team would heat it up. From then on, I enjoyed a hot meal every evening. While the rest of the ward had a packet of sandwiches and a yoghurt or a little tub of tinned fruit at 5pm, I would savour chilli-con-carne, curries and lovely pasta dishes. I was worried that it might cause a degree of jealousy with the other patients, but at the end of the day, Arianne told me to regard food as medicine. I had to eat my way out as well as rehab my way out of hospital.

The occupational therapy (OT) sessions were now in the OT gym which was in the Allied Health Professionals (AHP) hub area of the hospital. Cerys and Janine had already taught me over the preceding few weeks in ICU to relearn to use a knife and fork, and how to hold pencils and pens. They were very happy and full of life. I would see them coming into the ward and one of them would bring the wheelchair towards the bed with the other bringing the Stand Aid over. This was the cue for me to start to get ready. Initially, when I was bedbound, even getting to the point of sitting on the edge of the bed was a massive effort with one of the team helping me to swing my legs round before lifting my torso up. As time went on and I became stronger, I was shown how to do this move using the side of the bed and the weight of my upper body to lever my legs to the side. I also started to roll over in the bed myself and did not need to wait for two nurses to help me do this during the day and night.

Janine and Cerys were extremely patient at showing me how to get to the edge of the bed time after time and I had never thought that sitting on the edge of the bed would be so tricky. It was yet another thing that I had taken for granted until I became so ill. Fortunately, I mastered this reasonably well over the period of a few days and once the Stand Aid belt was placed around me, the routine of the machine providing a rising yet stable platform for my arms to help support my torso whilst I would drive weight through my legs and stand up became second nature. The machine could then be swung round and I would reverse the process to sit in the wheelchair. Either Janine or Cerys would take me to the lift, down two floors, along various corridors and we would arrive at the OT gym. The OT gym was excellent. It had large windows for capturing the light but, more importantly, a view of rolling hills and the River Tay. This gave me hope.

Once in the gym, there were numerous activities organised for me. The therapists were fascinated by the work involved in orthodontics and designed a bespoke daily programme of detailed skills-based activities similar to some of the routine tasks in orthodontics to help me regain the confidence in my ability to return to work. I would work on arm movements and hand control as well as sitting and standing. Various seated tasks and games would be set up from the gentle and delicate such as threading beads, lining up balls using tweezers and putting plumbing washers on hooks, through to the more energetic activities involving lifting and twisting, even on one occasion deconstructing and reassembling a hydraulic pump. I was fascinated by the boxes and boxes of materials that they had in the gym, along with larger objects and pieces of kit. Each was labelled and stored in exactly the right place. If only my office and garage were like that I thought.

On top of one of the rows of cupboards in the gym was a neat row of wooden stools and after several sessions, I asked why they were there. The answer was obvious, they had been made by former patients who were joiners and needed to relearn the skills required for carpentry. I wondered if there would be any occupation or job that would fox them.

The physiotherapists had a clear idea of what would be required for me to be discharged and to be safe at home. Not only would I have to be able to walk, but I would need to be safe walking on uneven ground, uphill/downhill, on stairs, and getting in and out of the car. The problem was that I hadn't done any of these activities for three months and I wondered how I would be able to do these again. There was to be no second place from now on. The team had a clear activity programme mapped and I was privileged to have such a wonderful team to look after me.

The physiotherapists took me to their gym at 3pm each day and, as with the OTs, we would have all sorts of conversations on the journey back and forth. The hospital was quiet during this period but on every journey we would meet someone I knew and it was great to meet familiar people and have a little chat. On reaching the gym, I always knew that it was time for business. The nasal cannula for oxygen would be changed to a mask to allow me to breathe oxygen through my mouth as well as through my nose. I was initially put through my paces by doing seated reaching exercises to help me with balance and strength. As the days elapsed, lifting exercises helped me develop improved arm movements and then leg exercises helped me to develop some early control of my legs. There were also standing exercises to help me gain confidence at standing and improving my balance. Each session lasted an hour and seemed to go by in a flash with the conversation and rest periods between the various activities.

The day finally came when walking was to be tried. It was day 96. I was very apprehensive as it brought back the memories of the first set of reaching exercises, being on the Tilt Table and using the Stand Aid. I need not have worried as Sophie and the team had everything under control. Everyone in the gym seemed excited and full of more enthusiasm than usual, if this would ever be possible. The Stand Aid machine was brought to the wheelchair, the belt was attached around me and up I went. There was no platform for my feet as they were on the ground. It felt slightly different but good. Louise kept the wheelchair behind me just in case. The team were encouraging me and as I took a step forwards with my left foot the machine was wheeled away by Steven. I made my first step in months. Next, I made a step with my right foot. Sophie was full of energy and asked me to take another step with my left foot. After 20 steps, I had to sit down on the wheelchair. It was the first time I had walked since becoming sick.

The only disappointment was that the camera had not worked. And so, the wheelchair was pushed back to the invisible start line and we repeated the steps. This time the camera worked and after another 20 steps, I was delighted. A glass of water was produced and I toasted the physiotherapy team. To me it tasted like the champagne of success that I had longed for since leaving ICU. It was short lived and was time to go back to the ward. Once back in bed, I uploaded the video to Facebook and watched the avalanche of generous and positive comments flood in. The best comment was from an old friend of 25 years who posted, 'One giant step for man...'. It truly did feel like I had made a major achievement in my rehabilitation journey. I texted Amanda and she was so happy that I had reached this point. It was a quiet evening and I went to sleep contented that the rehabilitation journey was going well.

The next day, I was keen to do some more walking in the physiotherapy gym and was ready for the afternoon session. The physiotherapists took me on the journey that by that point I knew so well and the Stand Aid machine was waiting again. I was duly strapped in, the arm rests rose up and I walked again but a slightly greater distance and repeated this a few more times. Over the next few days it started to feel increasingly normal until one day the Stand Aid was not in sight when the wheelchair reached the gym. In its place was a tall metal frame with padded armrests. This was known as a pulpit frame and I now had to reach up from the wheelchair and elevate my body to the standing position myself. It was a challenge but I made it. The pulpit frame was moved slowly forwards and I was again walking. This was used for several more days in the gym and a pulpit frame was found for me to use on the ward as well.

Then the big shock came. It was time to walk with only a Zimmer frame. It was uncomfortable to push the weight of my upper body through my arms and wrists onto the frame and simultaneously push this forwards but I was successful. This was repeated until I became increasingly confident. This was yet another step closer to independence. Learning to walk again was one of the biggest challenges of the journey and I was delighted to be at this point. I wanted more independence though and realised that practising the walking technique was as important as gaining the stamina to be able to walk longer distances so a Zimmer frame was provided for use on the ward. With help, I walked round the hospital ward, initially stopping for a rest, but eventually doing laps of the ward. I was also encouraged to use the Zimmer frame to transfer from the bed to the commode and to the wheelchair.

From then on, I made sure I was first in the shower after the domestics had cleaned it each day. I could see them cleaning the bathroom area from my bed as part of their early morning routine and once they were finished I would head over. I needed a towel so the challenge was to ask for a towel as the linen trolley was wheeled into the ward in the morning, gather my clothes and wash kit and head over using my Zimmer not only to walk, but also to hang my clothes on. The others in the bay joked about a personal best time, which amused me as I was in fact trying to speed up so that I would be reasonably quick and not a 'bog hogger' when I got home.

I had been taken past an area of the AHP hub over the weeks which intrigued me since it had a narrower door to the other areas. It turned out this was a flat that had been specifically designed with domestic-width doors and it had a bedroom, kitchen and bathroom. This was for the bedroom, kitchen and bathroom tests. These would need to be completed for me to be allowed home. Cerys and Janine asked me what I would like to make for lunch during the kitchen test. They asked if Amanda wanted to come in and this was scheduled for a few days later. Amanda came to the ward and then we all went to the kitchen and I set about making lunch. It was simple pasta dish and after I had opened all the packets and cans, Janine and Cerys left me to get on with it. I even managed to play the latest Andrea Bocelli concert to Amanda as we ate. Not the most romantic setting, but it was the best that I was going to be able to do as an in-patient.

Amanda was happy to help me tidy up and the kitchen test had been ticked off the list. I called my mum later and she told me that she found the kitchen test much easier when she had been in hospital a few years earlier for a large cancer operation, and then accused my two brothers and me of trying to have her deliberately failed by the OTs, so that she would be put in a nursing home! Nothing could be further from the truth. I was glad that we had now both been passed as kitchen safe. I knew I would have to persevere with the rehabilitation journey to return to being an active person. Forwards through rehabilitation was the only route to take.

The remaining test was the bathroom test. It was split into two parts. It was more than just washing and showering, it tested getting dressed. Janine took charge and observed and helped me wash by the bedside during one test, then supervised me in the shower during another. It reminded me of the dressing game we would play as kids for little squares of chocolate, only this time there was no prize, just the delight at now being able to have a shower on my own. It was another step closer to independence.

One Friday during the morning stretches, Sophie suggested that the stairs should be the next challenge. The physiotherapy gym has a set of four wooden stairs with a wooden banister and it so happened that Amanda was coming in to watch the afternoon session. The physiotherapists knew that the isolation of being an in-patient for so long was not good for either of us and had encouraged Amanda to participate in the rehabilitation journey as much as possible. Amanda met me in the gym and the stairs were duly brought out. I stood up from the wheelchair with the aid of the Zimmer frame and walked towards the stairs. Sophie went up the stairs to help catch me if I stumbled but it was no problem to put one foot in front of the other and ascend. I turned round and looked down. I have to admit I was anxious about falling as I went down but I could not show this and, again, Sophie was there in the event that I slipped and fell. It felt good to have achieved another goal and it was time to repeat the ascent and descent. This was all easy enough but the real test was the following Monday morning when Casey, Louise and Angela arrived at the bedside at 9am. It was time to use a flight of stairs to see how I would get on at home. Louise showed me how to go down backwards and forwards, take a break and then come back up. We did this three times that morning. I was glad to have completed this.

I was now eating, sleeping, rehabilitating and repeating, day after day. Everything was going in the right direction, except sleeping; I knew I needed to be at home for a good night's sleep.

———————

'DYING TO LIVE'

CHAPTER 13

New Horizons

I HAD A FEW sad days on the ward when I felt I was not making enough progress. On each of these occasions either Amanda or the rehabilitation team would boost me and remind me that the journey was long but that I had made an enormous amount of progress already and to keep going with the hard work. One Friday, I had been to physiotherapy with the usual energetic end of week afternoon session, the so-called 'big finish Friday', and was back on the ward. After nearly three and a half months, it hit me, *'How much longer would I be locked up for?'* Goal setting had become an essential for me and I didn't have a goal. I felt a bit down when speaking to Amanda that evening and I realised if I could have a rough date for discharge, then I would have the biggest goal of this phase of the rehabilitation journey to aim for. Having come out of being unconscious, I had originally been aiming for a maximum of six months in hospital, but wanted to beat this target.

I was resolute. On the Monday morning, I asked the ward doctor if we could discuss a discharge date during the ward round, which that day included Dr Andrews, the consultant, several junior doctors and Sophie. I asked my question about a potential discharge date for the weekend before Amanda returned to school. The team were all silent and Sophie broke the silence by saying, 'The patient doesn't set the discharge date,' which I understood. Dr Andrews let the team know that it was all down to the rehabilitation journey and that Sophie was the best person to determine when I would be ready for discharge. She suggested that if I could walk on smooth and rough ground, use the bathroom, shower, dress myself, use stairs and so on, then I would be fine for the discharge date that I wanted. I had by now ticked off much of the list, which was reassuring. I was made aware that the date might need to slip back if I was not ready and I accepted this. Sophie mentioned that if anyone would make this target, it would be me. She and the rest of the team laughed. I was delighted and the date was 'set'. There was a renewed sense of determination to conquer the remaining goals on my rehabilitation list. A week later, I discussed my next goal with Sophie and the physiotherapy team. There was a stunned silence when I stated that I wanted to walk out of the hospital on discharge day. Within a few minutes, Sophie broke the silence with, 'This was always the plan, you just didn't know it yet!' It was going to be a big challenge to walk the walk, rather than just talk about discharge day.

Although most rehabilitation sessions involved a degree of discomfort, the physiotherapists and OTs were incredible at motivation and driving me forward. They were truly inspirational and managed my body, mind and spirit even on the darkest days. I was constantly taken aback by their enthusiasm and inventiveness, even involving my wife and Sherlock Bones in some sessions. He had, of course, come in with Amanda one day when I was in ICU but he was to play a bigger part as I gained confidence in walking. Sophie, and from time to time the team, asked Amanda to bring him in for an outdoor physiotherapy session and duly I would be brought out from the ward to the front of the hospital. I realised this was all part of the discharge planning, which had started so many months ago. It was a case of bringing home into the hospital. Sophie had taken stock of everything either Amanda or I had told her and realised that Sherlock can be boisterous and could pull me off my feet. It was, therefore, important for him to get used to the wheelchair, walking stick, Zimmer frame and my slower pace of walking.

'DYING TO LIVE'

Naturally, as a young dog, he was interested in all the humans coming and going from the hospital but he was also listening and trying to be obedient. The therapists wanted him to pull on the lead, to make unpredictable movements, to bump into me, all in order to make me work hard to keep my balance. He wasn't there just for fun, he was now one of the rehabilitation team. I longed to walk in the woods near our house with him and knew that in time, this would be possible. It was now a matter of when, not if.

I was astonished at the incredible patience of the therapists and how they invested so much time and energy in me. They, along with the ICU nurses, showed me what 'care' really meant. The ward nurses had many more patients to look after and, therefore, there was much less one-to-one time. Hospital visiting was banned due to the risk of COVID-19 transmission throughout the first UK lockdown but was lifted two weeks after I moved to the ward. There was much discussion among the patients but I knew the rules were simple. Each patient would have one named visitor who could book a one-hour slot each day. No more than that. Sophie and the physiotherapists knew that part of my rehabilitation would require time for Amanda and I to be together on the ward but also in other places to speak about private and personal matters. They would organise clandestine outdoor physiotherapy sessions for me and hey presto, Amanda would magically appear in the 'same place at the same time'. The senior charge nurse got wind of this and had questioned Sophie and Angela about this but they stood their ground and let her know that it was an important part of the rehabilitation journey for a long-stay patient, and after all, I had nearly died so many times.

From this point on, the senior charge nurse was known affectionately as the Camp Commandant from the film, *The Great Escape*, and I was portrayed as Virgil Hilts, played by Steve McQueen as I felt I ended up in the cooler after each escape attempt. I don't think the Camp Commandant liked me from the moment a week or so earlier when Amanda and I had complained about the nursing ratio being too low for the number of high tariff patients and as a result I had to wait an hour for a urine bottle one day, ouch! I felt guilty that the nurses on duty that shift were given a row. Moreover, the Camp Commandant disliked the fact that I had to leave the ward so many times each day. The nurses became known as the Gestapo and it made light of the situation. I would joke endlessly with my friends that tunnelling was going well and that the Gestapo had no idea about the Tom, Dick and Harry tunnels. The metaphor of digging the tunnels and the rehabilitation tunnel was remarkably similar in my mind. *Would I get caught and be shot in any of the escape attempts?*

The physiotherapists each had their area of interest that they would work on. Angela was preoccupied with improving the functionality of my shoulders, particularly the right one which had been stiff and resistant to proper movement since the early days of waking up in ICU. It just wouldn't move as it was supposed to and, as a complex joint, it needed considerable mobilisation on an ongoing basis. Louise would focus on my legs when she was taking the lead. In ICU she helped me lift my weak legs in turn and later, when on the ward, worked with me to perform higher and higher hamstring stretches. She seemed obsessed to get them as near 90 degrees as possible and by the end of the in-patient phase, she was torturing her boyfriend with hamstring stretches as well. I felt a little guilty that my care was causing him a degree of discomfort of an evening as well.

Emily was one of the surprises in life. As a small stature physiotherapist, I was taken aback when one of the others in the team let me know that Emily was a rugby team coach and a Pilates trainer. I stopped asking any more questions when she told me that she had grown up on a farm and a fair bit of physical effort was the norm for her. Furthermore, Emily wanted to make my ankles and feet function as normally as possible and would gently, but thoroughly, manipulate them. Casey was the quiet dynamo in the team and would show me exercises to do in bed or by the bedside to rebuild my weak muscles whilst Katie was a cyclist and would be full of energy for every activity! Steven, who had come to see me one weekend in ICU was often in the background. A tall man with a sharp wit, he had many one-liners that could rival some stand-up comedians. He had the skill of being able to brighten any room just by entering. The team were exceptionally encouraging during my rehabilitation journey, with other physiotherapists helping when needed.

The Gestapo were mostly happy to accommodate Amanda visiting and would work around her schedule. As the weeks moved on, it suited Amanda to come in at 4pm most days and if she was able to join the physiotherapy session at 3pm, then she could spend two hours with me. The Gestapo had no idea about one particular 'escape' though. While in ICU, I had mentioned to Sophie and the team that it would be our wedding anniversary while I was in hospital and that, bearing in mind the events that Amanda had to go through, I felt it only reasonable to buy her an eternity ring this year. But how would I go about this? The physiotherapists were brilliant. They guided me through various jewellery catalogues on the tablet and helped me think through what would be most appropriate. I asked Anna to help me get the right size and finally remembered my credit card details and ordered the ring and had it delivered. The physiotherapists organised a lovely afternoon in the sunshine (I know how much trouble it was to fix the weather for us) and Amanda and I opened all our anniversary cards and shared our gifts. The Gestapo had no idea. Amanda wasn't too pleased when I suggested that she had now passed the 'sickness and in health' challenge.

The Gestapo did have their work cut out though. Not only were they nursing some very sick patients, some of whom would end up dying from such conditions as chronic obstructive pulmonary disease (COPD) and lung cancer, they would have to help the relatives during the most horrendous time. I was initially next to a wonderful man, Tom, who in his sixties was permanently on oxygen therapy and lived downstairs in his house as he was too unwell to make it upstairs. He rarely went out and had been in and out of hospital so many times with COPD and wondered if this would be the last time.

Robin left the hospital shortly after to a great deal of applause in the corridor. It was great to see him go home. He was the oldest survivor of COVID in the hospital. On the morning he left, he told me to work hard with the 'angels' as he called the physiotherapists. Another gentleman was moved in to be next to me for many weeks. Alex was in his eighties and had COPD. He and his wife had moved from a house to a flat because of his illness. Alex would sleep with his eyes wide open and, on more than one occasion, I thought he had died. He, like Robin, had lived a great life and had many tales to tell but was now a shadow of his former self and was restricted in every way by his condition. How sad for Alex and his wife I thought, especially when he was readmitted a second time and seemed to be going downhill rapidly. Death seemed to be a regular occurrence in the ward with patients discussing this openly with their consultants and the signing of 'do not resuscitate' certificates on admission. I never saw anybody die but I knew it was coming when the morphine pump was set up and the patient moved to a side-room when one became available. It was sad to see their name rubbed out from the door when they had passed away. I recalled working in hospitals over the years and hearing the porters wheeling a mortuary trolley to collect a body, a so-called 'Ward 13 call', with the empty trolley rattling whilst the full trolley on return making much less noise. It struck me how lucky I had been and how important it was to me to make a full recovery.

The long-suffering Gestapo had to undertake a degree of crowd control as well as nursing some very sick and terminally-ill patients. There were some interesting patients. One noisy night, an elderly gentleman was admitted and caused chaos from then till dawn: shouting and arguing, cussing and misogynistic, just like Father Jack in the TV comedy *Father Ted*, wanting to go to the bathroom, even with a catheter. In the end he fell asleep before the end of the night and slept most of the next day. I knew Father Jack was psychotic as this would go on night after night, but I wondered if my mental health would be compromised by my long stay in hospital. A regular patient in the ward was Dave. He had no idea of day or night and would constantly call for his wife. He would wake me up during the night sometimes standing next to my bed asking me if I would get him a pint from the bar or go to the football with him. If only! Another patient also called David wanted to jump out of the window constantly. I nicknamed him 'Dangerous Dave'. He was also convinced the marines were hiding in the trees outside and were going to storm the building. It was an interesting time. There was also Connor who had a tooth in his lung. It had been punched down his throat in a fight and he was having surgery for it to be removed. Connor, like so many others were sadly on methadone. He broke the rules and was rolling cannabis joints under the bedclothes and kept sneaking out for a smoke. He was eventually caught and was restricted to bed but had also been concealing a bottle of methadone from home and was double-dosing when the nurses administered each hospital dose. He was found out on this account too. The finale came when he coughed up the tooth at 4am one night. I can't say I shared his happiness at this point and I wondered if his manner might have contributed to his predicament in the first place.

The ward was an eye opener and the Gestapo had their work cut out. At one stage I was the only patient in the bay not on methadone and, at another juncture, was the only patient not called David. Five Davids all in the one place. One was full of life, even though he was waiting for a bed in a palliative care unit as he too was dying of lung cancer. He was a gambler and had encouraged some of the others in the bay to bet on the horse racing with him and his named visitor. Gambling on the horses isn't my scene but I decided to do some share dealing and was several hundreds of pounds better off while he seemed to lose small amounts of money every day. I was sorry to see him leave as he was a real character but the ambulance crew did at least take him for a lap of honour to say goodbye to everyone on what would be his penultimate journey. The Gestapo also had to deal with strange incidents and foul language on a regular basis. I had to listen to and witness a side of life that was somewhat alien to me and it was a pleasure to escape the ward several times each day for rehabilitation activities as well as several secret rendezvous with Amanda from time to time.

I had a further CT scan on day 102 and one of my consultant colleagues, Dr Foster, who I knew fairly well from various hospital meetings, was keen to show me the results and talk through the implications. The X-ray software wasn't behaving properly so one of the younger doctors was asked to intervene. The CT that was taken when I was at my most sick stage was brought up and Dr Foster stated 'incompatible with life'. I appreciated his honesty and the latest scan was put on the screen. He shared with me that whilst there was good news in that my lungs had improved substantially, considerable fibrosis and structural damage was present and this might not recover. I would from now on be managed in a similar manner to a patient with COPD. The difficulty was that nobody had an end point to aim for with COVID-19 being a new disease. It seemed strange that I no longer had a goal to aim for even though stepwise goal-setting had been such an important feature of the rehabilitation journey so far. I thought about this over a day or two and decided that whilst my lungs were unlikely to reach 100% ever again, I would settle for 50%.

The oxygen support was gradually reduced and on day 107, was stopped. I was finally totally free of all lines and tubes. It was one of the long term goals and I was glad to be at this point. It felt strange but freedom felt so good and I could now move at will. No longer would I have to be reconnected to the oxygen in the bathroom or

'DYING TO LIVE'

shower room and could go alone, nor would I need an oxygen cylinder and mask for the gym, making the sessions more productive.

The rehabilitation continued to step up and the enthusiasm of the therapists was infectious. They had decided earlier that as I had been a patient in hospital for so long that the integration with home life would take some time so home was to be brought into the hospital. Amanda was asked for a map of the house, a walk through video of the main rooms I would use on discharge and to measure all of the sofas and chairs I would sit on at home, the height of our bed, the exact make of car in which I would travel home and in which I would travel to appointments over the next weeks, the height of the toilet from the floor, the number of stairs into the house and from the living room to our bedroom and bathroom. As I now had more control of my head and limbs, I no longer required such a supportive wheelchair and this was replaced with a much smaller version that could be easily folded to go in the car. Various aids were ordered for the bathroom to help me use the toilet and shower safely and a stool for the kitchen to allow me to perch at the worktop and cooker without tiring. This had all been orchestrated precisely so that these were at home when I would arrive. The final days of rehabilitation in the hospital involved all sorts of interesting games in the occupational therapy gym, obstacle courses in the physiotherapy gym, along with practising getting in and out of a pretend car made from a rowing machine and various pieces of gym equipment.

As discharge day approached, the occupational therapy activities accelerated. A box of objects with tennis balls to roll on a table, paper clips to link, clothes pegs to put on a cup and putty to squeeze and knead was loaned to me to help me work on hand and arm movements at home. These were techniques used for patients recovering from a stroke. How glad I was that I had not suffered a stroke but I knew the rehabilitation of my hand and arm function would take time and perseverance. There were a number of activities that I would also need to undertake safely at home.

By now, I had been accessing my work emails and had found over 17,000 unread messages in my inbox. I was cognitively ready to start working. It would take some time to go through them but I decided to read the emails as they arrived each day. This would help me keep up-to-date with what was happening at work, and after all, everything had been turned upside down by COVID-19 and I would have to get up to speed. One email was about this week's Grand Rounds in the hospital, in which either a consultant or senior academic staff member delivered a presentation on a topic of importance or interest. This week it was Kunal's brother from Boston, USA, who was speaking on cardiothoracic surgery. He is a world expert and it was a coup to have him speak in my backyard. He had been due to come to the hospital this summer as his daughter was to be undertaking a student exchange with us, but this had not gone ahead. I texted Kunal to see if he could find a computer for me to watch the now online lecture being delivered from Boston.

Kunal had me dropped off in my wheelchair after my occupational therapy session in the morning and I had the pleasure of joining the whole oral and maxillofacial surgery department for a fast-food lunch. I was back with my friends and colleagues and it felt good. Interestingly, Kunal's brother spoke at one point about ECMO and although it was challenging to keep my composure, it was interesting to hear about the technique developed by his predecessor in his world-class cardiothoracic unit, which had now also saved my life. The importance of this technique resonated there and then. Many people, including myself, would not be alive now without medical pioneers. Kunal and Sam pushed me back to the ward and although they had been prevented from coming to see me by the Gestapo on many occasions, they now had a valid reason to be in the ward. We all laughed like small boys and it was fun to be helped back to my bed by them. Once settled, they made a hasty exit in case the Gestapo found them. The next day, my other department colleague Timothy texted me to let me know that he was around and wanted to meet Amanda and me at the end of the working day with his wife for more fast food. We shared a lovely hour in the hospital foyer chatting and eating a burger – how bourgeois!

The hospital had been approached by BBC Scotland and Scottish Television for a respiratory consultant and a patient to appear on the TV news in a story about ECMO and the respiratory impact of COVID-19. My journey was unique and as a long-term patient who had survived relatively unscathed from so many close shaves, I was asked to participate in the TV interviews along with Amanda. It was a pleasure to thank the 200-plus people who had cared for both me and my family so well. BBC Scotland had collected so much information that they ran a website story on the life and death knife-edge aspect of ECMO and the gruelling nature of surviving the ECMO journey specifically. It was strange to see Amanda and me on the TV and on the BBC news website. The STV story was also run on their website and the Scottish First Minister re-tweeted it on Twitter with an accompanying get-well message, which was thoughtful.

As the planned discharge day drew ever closer, the horizon drew ever closer and the light at the end of the metaphorical tunnel shone brighter. I would walk round the ward with my walking stick many, many times each day to improve my stamina. I knew this would take time, but each step was a step closer to my final recovery goal. I had by now decided that this was not going to be the life that I left, but the life that I now wanted to live, the new normal. Sophie and her team encouraged me to walk as far as possible in the hospital, and in the physiotherapy department on the penultimate day, the team had me walking laps of the department as well. My feet were sore and I put this down to the distance I had walked.

Day 128 finally came. It was the day we had all been working towards. And what a day it was to be, I would make the great escape and this time there would be no cooler. I was finally going to be discharged from hospital and return home to my 'natural habitat'. I was aware that I had become institutionalised and I needed to return to my normal routines, except that normal life had changed due to COVID-19. Everyone's lives had changed. I didn't know how the world had changed even though I had heard the nurses talking about their daily lives and what aspects were now different. More worryingly, I didn't know how much of a return to normal health I would make and this concerned me.

As I woke up that morning, I reflected on the journey my family and I had made over the previous four months. Everything and everyone had been focussed on my survival and initial recovery but what about my wife and family? *Who had been looking after them? How had they coped and what had they experienced during this difficult period?* These were questions that I now needed answered along with other, perhaps lesser, issues that were on my mind. *What was the garden like? How much money did we have in the bank now for our bills? Could we go on a 'normal' holiday again? How would it feel to be back around our adult children after so long? How was my mother coping with the situation?* Clearly COVID-19 had taken a toll on our extended family and friends and I needed to get to know everyone again.

One thing I had decided during my time in hospital was that being locked away from family and friends had been an ordeal and that, after everyone's generosity in keeping in touch with me, I now needed to make more effort when I returned home to keep in touch with them. I had decided that I should try and meet up with someone at least once per week and resolved to be a better husband, father, brother and friend. Never had I missed the contact with others so much and whilst the hospital staff and other patients had been generous with their time towards me, it was my turn to offer something in return to the people who had helped me through.

Suddenly, the curtains next to me were opened by the nurse, Liz. The sun was shining and I knew it was going to be a happy day.

Liz came and had a chat with me as she had done on many mornings before. She knew it was my last day and brought me a cup of tea. It was a simple but lovely gesture to help me start my last day and she told me that the staff never hug patients but if she could, she would. I was touched. The other patients in the bay started to wake up and the usual chatter among the patients got going. I knew I had shared the hospital with some interesting patients, others with complex medical needs, some with very challenging behaviour, those that were pleasant, rude, deranged, happy and those at the end of life. I spent some time thinking about the patients who were less fortunate than me. What had happened to Edith, Billy, Tom, Alex, Dave, Dangerous Dave and all the other Davids along with Connor from the ward? I also thought about the other COVID-19 patients who had died. Today was to be the happiest of days for our family but for me there was an air of sadness too that others had not survived and, while we would celebrate, other families would be wrapped in grief. I was glad to have made it to this part of the journey and gave thanks for the input of everyone.

———————

CHAPTER 14

The Home Run

'EAT, SLEEP, REHAB AND REPEAT.' These were the words I had kept saying to myself in the weeks leading up to discharge from the hospital. I had joked with the physiotherapists that it would make a great T-shirt so I had decided one evening while lying in bed to have it made. The T-shirt accordingly arrived in good time.

I got up swiftly that morning to ensure there would be no delays. I was first in the bathroom and shower as ever and put on my new T-shirt, which amused the nursing staff on the ward. There was a gentle air of celebration around the ward while the medicines were being distributed and breakfast was being organised. It would be the last time I would savour the strawberries that Amanda had brought in to top my porridge. Many of the nurses and other staff in the ward and beyond came to see me to wish me well. I knew they had worked so hard to revive me and that my body had given them so many worries but also that each step forward for me was another step forward for everyone.

Deborah, the ICU liaison nurse, and Dr Morris, the ICU consultant, were some of the visitors that morning. It was a great opportunity to thank them both for everything they had done. After all, they had brought me back from near-death on multiple occasions and had been caring for me in the darkest of times. We had a frank and open conversation about my time in hospital and the transition to home. Dr Morris told me that she was amazed I had made it through and had often thought I had no chance of survival.

She felt it was a miracle that I had survived. I explained that my inner strength primarily came from my mother who has survived many tough times in her life, including bowel cancer. Almost immediately after her major operation to remove the cancer she was back to her old self, and I suspected my ability to have survived the toughest of times was down to the genes from her. Dr Morris told me that the doctors wanted to know what was inside me and if they could tap into the 'core of steel'. I was delighted that the medical team felt that I perhaps had some form of inner strength to be able to have survived COVID-19 and the complications that had emanated from the initial time in hospital. I didn't want to use the word miracle as many friends and family had suggested but to hear this word mentioned by medical and nursing staff was incredible, if not surprising.

The core of steel was of course down to my clan motto, *per ardua*. On its own, it is of limited value but working alongside the wonderful knowledge and skill of the doctors, the dedication of the nursing teams, sheer brilliance of the rehabilitation team, the power of prayer, support of friends, family and colleagues, and perhaps a bit of luck as well, the medical team had not only kept me alive but had renewed me. I took some time to give thanks to God for being a survivor, but of more concern to me was that so many people were still becoming sick and that so many were dying. I would remember all those who had died and their grieving relatives in my own prayers.

I realised that I had become reliant on the daily routine in the ward and that home would be so different. I had met all of the key goals I had set myself in recent months. I could put on my socks, I could draw, write, stand, talk and walk. Work, golf, skiing and motorcycling would need to wait for now but I was safe to return home. The nursing staff were brilliant at getting me ready for home as well. My drugs were readied and I was taken through what to take and when. I was shown how to use and clean the nebuliser and the constituent parts. Darth Vader in a phone box was coming home with me. I had various conversations with others on the ward who had by now worked out that there was going to be a celebration for me leaving. Amanda arrived with a bag for all my clothes, various books and items of electronic equipment. It amazed me that for four months, my life had been relatively simple and everything I needed was in one small cupboard and on one table. I had clothes, food and drink along with entertainment in the form of books and a tablet, mobile phone and headphones along with various chargers. There were games and children's toys that some of the consultants had bought for me to help me start using my hands again after I had regained consciousness. These would remain in the hospital for other patients to use. Not surprisingly the bag was not big enough so an additional bag was needed for clothing.

The physiotherapists and OTs who had been the centre of my routine for such a long time while in hospital all arrived well before the duly appointed leaving time. They loved the T-shirt. I was humbled when they insisted I sit on the bed and they produced a card and a present for me. How thoughtful. The card had been signed by them all with individual messages and I was truly touched. It was a card to be treasured. The book was very interesting. It chronicled a similar journey to mine and a lot of thought had gone into its purchase. I was humbled. The physiotherapists and OTs had been with me from the first day in hospital till now and it was time to say goodbye to the majority of this amazing team. I knew that now was not the time for tears even though goodbyes are hard. Now was the time to show the team what we had all been aiming for: discharge to home for the next stage of my recovery, recuperation and rehabilitation (stage 4). The Zimmer frame was not coming home with us. Yes, I would need support and assistance to get around but I did not want to be burdened with equipment that I would not use. In any case, it would not fit in the car so it was agreed to leave it behind. The physiotherapists would kindly return it to the store and someone else could make use of it.

'DYING TO LIVE'

It was time to go. Now was the time to leave behind the little world that had become the normal for me - Bed 3, Bay 3, Ward 3. How strange. Even stranger was the fact that Sophie had shared with me: I had spent a total of 42 days on active ECMO, 42 days in ICU and the discharge date I had originally chosen to allow a weekend at home with Amanda before she went back to school would have been 42 days in the ward. This was brought forward to a Thursday to allow a visit by Sophie on the Friday. I told myself that going home would be a pleasure and it had been my desire to walk out of the ward and give the staff something to celebrate.

Jana, one of the happiest nurses I had met during my journey gave me a hug. I was slightly embarrassed but thankful nevertheless. I picked up the piece of paper where I had written a few words in case there was the opportunity to speak outside.

I was ready and it was time to shine. I walked out of the ward to rapturous applause and saw so many of the kind-hearted staff that had cared for me so well over the previous months. I had a glide in my stride. It was the equivalent of a child leaving a hospital cancer ward and ringing the bell with all the staff cheering. I didn't know it at the time but the news reports had carried stories of many other COVID-19 patients being clapped out of hospital and looking back, I am delighted that so many people have had the same phenomenal experience. Along with the staff who had cared for me were many colleagues from the hospital who, along with my family and friends, had worried and prayed for me continually. I was ecstatic at seeing them all in the same place. It was absolutely joyous. I had said to the physiotherapists two weeks before leaving that I did not want to leave in a wheelchair and in my head, having been wheeled in on a stretcher to hospital several months earlier, I wanted to walk out as a sign to myself at least that I had made considerable progress in my recovery so far. I didn't bargain for the sheer number of people clapping me out. I had no difficulty walking the walk and at one point raised my stick in the air to celebrate with some close colleagues that I spotted. This moment was caught on camera along with the T-shirt.

The corridor seemed to go on and on but I knew I could do it as we had done a trial walk the week before with Sophie. The wheelchair was being pushed behind me as a backup but there was no way I was going to use it until we reached the end of the corridor. I even managed a short speech thanking everyone at the end of the corridor. It was the least I could do. The whole event had been recorded by the hospital communications team and was published on social media later in the day. Little did I know that this would go viral again. Amanda went to fetch the car and my colleague and friend Sam spoke to me whilst I waited with the rehabilitation team. He, in true Sir Lancelot Spratt style, had parked his flash car at the hospital entrance and zoomed off just before the parking warden issued another fine. He was renowned in the hospital for accruing parking fines and at one point, years before, the bailiffs had been chasing him. At least some things never change, I mused.

There was the opportunity for a socially-distanced photograph with the rehabilitation team at the hospital entrance. This was used by some of the media the next day in their coverage of me leaving hospital. The 'sickest survivor' had now made it to discharge! I knew I would miss the rehabilitation team but as one door closes in life, another opens. I bumped into other colleagues who were going into the hospital to do an operating theatre list and it was great to see them. Amanda and the rehabilitation team helped me into the car. It was easier than expected and we set off for home. It was a pleasant journey driving past the farms and buildings I recognised so well. At least this time I knew there was no chance of returning to the hospital, except in a few months for follow-up appointments.

We stopped in our village for bread. I waited in the car and enjoyed the sun warming the car while I waited for Amanda to return. My phone had been buzzing like a bee with messages all morning and continued to do so. I was buoyed by so many messages congratulating me on leaving hospital but I knew that I still had to get into the house. Amanda returned and sent a quick message. We travelled the last few miles home and there waiting was a surprisingly large crowd of close family, good friends and neighbours all waving flags and clapping me home.

I hadn't seen my family for four months and it was slightly overwhelming. The sun kept warming me like a heat lamp as I got out of the car but I was pretty tired. I needed to get into the house for a rest. There, waiting for me at the back door, was a piece of red carpet that glinted like a ruby in the sunshine – found by my good friend Piers in our garage. I laughed and went inside and sat down, but not until he took another photo of me for social media. Sherlock had wondered what was going on and bounded over to see me. This time, there was no confusion, he knew I was home. It was a relief to relax for a few minutes and stroke Sherlock. He was now my 'therapet'.

I went out to the patio at the back and it had been decorated in true 'welcome home' style; a buffet lunch was sitting ready to go. I sat outside with Amanda and those closest to us to enjoy lunch in the sun. What a treat. This was the day we had been planning for over many weeks and it felt good to be finally at home. It was a lovely hour or so after which I knew I was done for the day. It was time to head back inside for a snooze and to regain some energy. I could finally have a nap in my own bed. Compared to the air mattress in the hospital bed, my goodness, it was rock hard and I realised that I had a long way to go in order to rebuild what I had lost. My back was all bones and offered little protection. I got up later in the afternoon and had dinner round the table for the first time with my family in over four months. I think this was as important for them as it was for me. My request was macaroni and cheese, something I had craved during my time in hospital and Amanda's cheese sauce was smooth and, well cheesy, unlike the NHS cheese sauce. I didn't sleep particularly well the first night I was home but I didn't care, I was home.

The T-shirt seemed to catch the eye of the media along with the official media release and the phone started ringing with journalists wanting the story of our family's COVID-19 journey and our experiences. I was not used to the limelight or the media and had no training in this area but was fortunate that the hospital communications team managed this for me as an employee and took care of all the formalities. The newspapers wanted to go to print relatively quickly so the interviews were speedy. A photographer was dispatched to the house by one of the large publishers and various shots were taken. I was again on the front pages and in the middle of several newspapers, serialised across various other titles. I also did various radio interviews and it was odd to go out in the car the next day and hear myself on the news bulletin speaking about my condition and treatment. I also recognised a story of the 'sickest survivor' on the all-staff email the next day and later in the month, I was delighted to read in the NHS Board minutes that the Board had wished me well with the rest of my recovery.

I was among the group of patients across the UK who had spent a considerable amount of time in hospital and, within this, a substantial time being ventilated. There were only two other Scottish patients in the media spotlight, Robin, my COVID-19 friend from ICU and the ward, who had spent 91 days in hospital in total, and another patient in Lanarkshire, Stephen Cameron, 'patient 91', a pilot who fell ill in Vietnam and spent 65 days on life support before being transferred back to Scotland. The three of us were the most severe cases that had survived. Amanda heard of another patient who had been in hospital for longer than me in another part of Scotland, but we later heard that he had sadly died.

The hospital put the story and video on social media as well. There were 800,000 views and over 200 comments from a combination of well-wishers (the majority) and a few critics/trolls. The well-wishers were very kind with many congratulating me on getting to this point and others noting the excellent care the NHS provides, free at the point of delivery. Some estimated my bill to this point in the USA would be over $1.1 million, which shocked me. Just as well I pay my taxes, I thought. I am used to criticism as everything we publish in research journals undergoes peer-review where two or more people review our work and suggest areas for improvement. I also participate in this process and like to point out how these flaws can be addressed, but I was not ready for the amount of negativity on social media. Idiots from across the globe feel it is their right to vent their minds online, irrespective of the hurt they might cause. A number of comments referred to me as some sort of paid actor working on an NHS publicity film, others asked why the doctors and nurses were standing around clapping when they should have been working instead. Yet others criticised my length of 'hotel' stay or the fact that I was not wearing a mask when leaving the hospital. At this point, my breathing was too poor for me to walk with a mask. How frustrating.

I became aware that David Icke, the former sports commentator, had claimed in a YouTube video at the start of the pandemic in the UK that COVID-19 was linked to 5G mobile phone networks. Icke later said in an interview on an internet TV channel that Israel was using the pandemic 'to test its technology' and any attempt to expect people to become vaccinated amounted to 'fascism'. He also claimed, 'If 5G continues and reaches where they want to take it, human life as we know it is over. . . so people have to make a decision'. The YouTube video was removed and the platform tightened their rules to prevent it from being used to spread unsubstantiated theories. It was then deleted by Facebook. Icke's Facebook page and YouTube channel were deleted in May 2020. Even though it is not biologically possible for a virus to be spread by the electromagnetic spectrum, this seemed to be an ongoing theory and I received many messages on social media asking where my nearest mast was. Living out in the country, we are many miles from a 5G mast.

Other comments I received were that COVID-19 was not a real disease and I was a fake. At the centre of this myth is David Icke again, who spoke at an anti-lockdown protest in Trafalgar Square in London in August 2020, organised by the group Unite for Freedom. Icke claimed, 'Anyone with a half a brain cell on active duty can see coronavirus is nonsense' and, 'We have a virus so intelligent that it only infects those taking part in protests the government wants to stop'. He further said, 'This world is controlled by a tiny few people' who 'impose their agenda on billions of people.' He then turned to the attending police at the rally and insulted them by saying they were 'enforcing fascism that your own children will have to live with.' He went on to ask the police to 'join us and stop serving the psychopaths.' Early in November 2020, Twitter permanently suspended Icke's account for violations regarding misinformation. To call COVID-19 a myth insults those who have lost loved ones due to a horrific disease.

Other keyboard 'doctors' came up with all sorts of cures that would clearly have prevented me from suffering so badly, such as homeopathic remedies from Aboriginal tree roots and of course Ivermectin, Chloroquine, Remdesevir, silver solution, UV skin radiation, megadose vitamin D and, Donald Trump's favourite, a bleach kit. I decided that my job was not to accept the garbage being spouted by these individuals but to reply to each and every detractor, pointing out the evidence for and against their weird and wonderful preventive strategies and remedies. After all, I now had more time on my hands than the trolls had energy. It took many weeks to continually reply to everyone but in the end, they either accepted my evidence-based information or gave up.

The morning after returning home allowed a quiet breakfast for Amanda and me and I managed to get round the house reasonably well. It was tiring though. Sophie did a home visit in the afternoon to check that all was well. We did some gentle stretching and then, as ever, Sophie challenged me to walk a little up our road to make sure that I wouldn't become housebound. This was an excellent strategy and although I was slow, I made it there and back. I was pleased with my effort. I now had the OT box and my physiotherapy stretches and exercises to do myself each day. I became disciplined to do these first thing each morning.

I was conscious that in the news, hundreds in the UK marched for fair pay for NHS workers due to the pressures of their jobs in the previous five months. I for one would have fully supported this move as someone who has not only worked in the NHS for nearly 30 years, but who has seen at first hand the knowledge, skill and intensity of work that is involved with many jobs in the NHS. Doctors are expected to know everything, nurses now do many of the roles that doctors used to do and have increasing numbers of patients with increasingly complex needs to look after whilst the AHP team provide essential services that restore, rehabilitate and reinvigorate those recovering from disease or injury as well as the weak and the weary, the sad and the lonely.

I felt I had been running a marathon every day and I was glad to be at home with Amanda and my family. I no longer had the security of the hospital regime to rely on, but I felt a sense of privilege having met so many exceptional NHS staff and having been given the opportunity to have had many positive experiences as an ICU and ward patient. The various staff members had each played their part in my journey with the regular contact from family, friends and so many people in dentistry and orthodontics continually boosting my spirits.

The world was still in turmoil even though I had made a home run. There was work to do, recovery would take many more months of hard work.

PHOTOGRAPHS

SECTION TWO

16 — Amanda, Sherlock Bones and me ready
for an outdoor physiotherapy session.

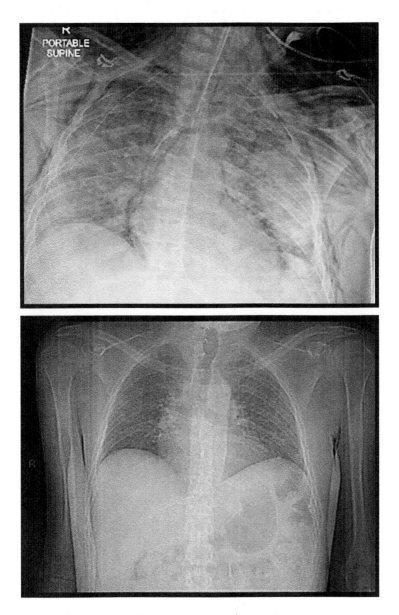

17 — My CT scans. *Top*, at day 15 showing
95% pneumonia and only 5% lung capacity for breathing;
and *above*, showing a massive improvement on day 102.

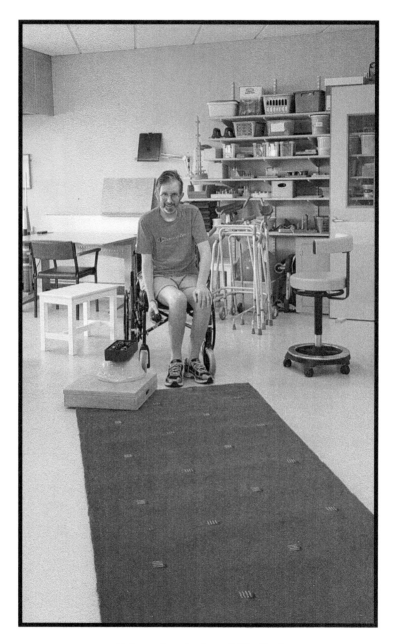

18 — Relearning the key skill of balance
by playing carpet bowls.

19 — Relearning coordination by putting using a golf club.

Scotland

ECMO - The Covid patient who got the most intensive care

By Susie Forrest
Scottish health producer, BBC News

31 July 2020

Coronavirus pandemic

Grant McIntyre does not remember anything for 50 days while he was receiving ECMO treatment

20 — TV and media coverage of the ECMO journey and the story to this point.

21 — More media coverage.

22 — A socially-distanced photograph on discharge day,
with the rehabilitation team.

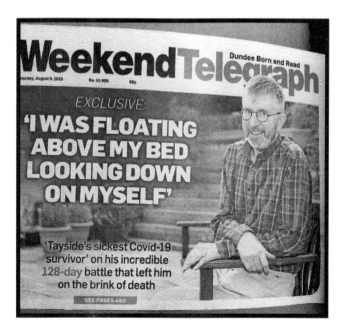

23 — Front page of one of our local newspapers
a few days following discharge.

24 — My nebuliser, used morning and night
for eight weeks in total.

25 – Sherlock Bones and his new brother, Watson, who joined
our family as my rehabilitation journey continued.

26 – Learning to ride a bike again.

27 — My 'kitchen' physiotherapy and
occupational therapy gym.

28 — Our first trip out for dinner as a couple.

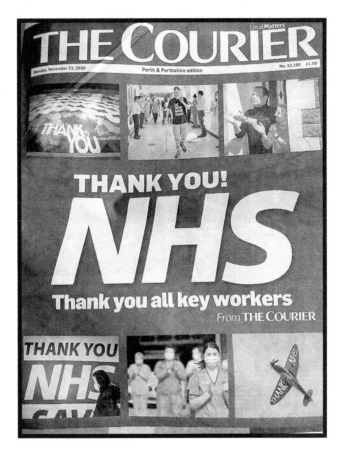

29 — One of our local papers thanking the key workers for their hard work during 2020. I for one wouldn't be in the fortunate position of returning to normal without the input and support of so many people.

CHAPTER 15

The Next Steps

The world was recovering from the first COVID-19 wave as summer 2020 turned to autumn. Earlier in the year, a second wave had also been suggested as likely to affect the UK and everyone was hoping that their fears would be unfounded. Japan had already experienced a second wave. Sensibly, the WHO published updated guidance on masks, recommending that children over the age of 12 should abide by the same rules as adults. Masks and social distancing are the two most important public health measures to prevent transmission of a preventable disease. The virus can't jump from person-to-person unless it is transmitted via droplet or aerosol spread such as breathing, coughing or sneezing.

Sadly, the global death toll continued to increase, with local and national lockdowns announced in many countries. This led to civic unrest with large protests held in many European capitals. August was fortunately a quiet month in the UK in COVID-19 terms with people encouraged to use the 'Eat Out to Help Out' scheme to reinvigorate the hospitality industry. It was colloquially renamed 'Eat Out to Spread it About' as people enjoyed the freedoms that had been missing from the months before and the weather was good. I also enjoyed freedom, relatively speaking. I was just out of hospital and I knew there were many steps to be taken before I would get back to normal.

The second wave of infection that hit the UK was not a surprise. Rather than taking the brave and bold step of a full UK lockdown, the tiers and levels system introduced instead failed spectacularly. These resulted in over 65 changes in the rules relating to daily life not to mention travel. Whilst the UK political administrations jockeyed with each other to showcase their strategy as being better than the others, they failed to acknowledge that the UK, collectively, had become, according to the league table for transmission and death, the worst country in the developed world over the winter of 2021. How sad that our political leaders used the population as pawns in a game of chess rather than addressing the underlying issues. These were clear to me: confusing and ever-changing government advice, people not following instructions and no real penalties for failing to follow these, whilst so many shops, hospitality venues and schools remained open. These provided the ideal vector for transmission. To say that I was angry that the second wave was worse than the first, is an understatement. Brexit should have been halted and the UK should have worked with European partners to eradicate the disease.

For the following few weeks, either Sophie or Louise would come to the house twice a week and it was lovely to see them. After all, they had been such an important part of the months I had spent in hospital and they linked me with that period of my life. I transitioned to community-based occupational therapy and physiotherapy services which initially did house calls and helped me with my home exercise programme. The first day I met Kathryn, my new community physiotherapist, was during one of the sessions with Sophie. I discovered fairly quickly that Kathryn and Sophie were similar in nature and although they did things slightly differently, they had the same expectations for my ongoing treatment, focusing on increasing my mobility and independence, physical ability and my personal goals. Like the other physio-therapists, Kathryn would not take 'no' for an answer and I was only allowed to say 'not now' on a few occasions. Like Sophie, Kathryn was the 'Boss' in the community team and I was privileged to be in their care with their combined wisdom and experience. Both worked hard to get the best out of me and the best for me.

I got into a routine with Kathryn who always managed to come on a sunny afternoon. She encouraged me to make use of the house structures as a gym. I used the kitchen worktop for stretching my back, a pulley over a door for stretching my shoulders, leg weights for my quadriceps muscles, did press-ups against a door to exercise my arms and exercised with a gym ball that Anna had found in a cupboard from her days in dancing. I would side-step back and forth in the kitchen and reach into high cupboards as further stretching exercises. I was no athlete, more of a welterweight doing ballet dancing. In addition, I went for a daily walk with Sherlock and either Amanda, Anna and her partner Lawrence, or Colin. Sherlock became my rehab companion and gradually I stretched the distance I walked every day. My joints still ached, which I viewed as part of the recovery process. With the help of my friends taking me out for coffees and lunches, I gradually became less reliant on the wheelchair and was able to walk on level surfaces more easily. I was lucky to have a disabled parking permit to allow me to get closer to the destination each time I was taken out somewhere and could then walk to the venue a little without being overly breathless.

Being home was great and I made sure I continued to keep in contact with the family, friends and colleagues who had been so kind over the preceding months. I was not able to drive at this point and relied on people coming to see me or to take me out. My good friends, Piers, Drew and Darryl, were relatively selfless in this regard as were our neighbourly friends across the road who would come and cut the grass for us without asking. I did eventually cut the front grass myself a month or so after coming out of hospital, but it took a whole morning and it was no bowling green at the end. I was burned out for the rest of the day. I now knew what tiredness meant!

Medically, there were few breakthroughs as autumn unfolded, everything hinged on geopolitics. President Trump announced emergency authorisation for a new blood plasma treatment for

COVID-19 patients, despite no conclusive evidence about its effectiveness. The US refused to join COVAX, an international effort organised by the WHO to collectively create and distribute a vaccine. In one of many stupid outbursts, Trump claimed that COVID-19 would 'go away' through 'herd mentality' even as India had passed 5 million cases and France was about to experience a new record for the country with over 10,000 daily cases. Nothing about Donald Trump seemed to shock the world anymore. His inability to listen to scientists and doctors was a significant contributor to the horrific transmission and death figures in the US. Facebook and Twitter later took action against posts by Trump that compared COVID-19 to the flu. Although Facebook went on to declare that it would not remove anti-vaccine posts, YouTube announced it would remove anti-coronavirus vaccine content from the site. The White House listed 'Ending the COVID-19 pandemic' as one of President Trump's accomplishments, despite at the end of October nearly half a million Americans testing positive for Covid-19 in a week.

My breathlessness slowly improved with gentle exercise and I was pleased with this. Kathryn gradually increased the intensity of exercise. She was able to read me easily, and she discovered fairly quickly that I was prepared to continue to put in the rehabilitation effort but needed structure and motivation. Like most people I have these in abundance for the things that I want to do but had lacked the motivation to do regular exercise for many years. Perhaps now would be the time for this to change and Kathryn wisely used this opportunity to encourage me to modify my views on exercise and was able to invoke a degree of enthusiasm.

Education had suffered in the UK with the majority of children having been taught remotely in spring 2020. The UK Chief Medical Officers published a statement that children were at low risk of contracting and dying from COVID-19. Sadly, the statement said nothing about silent transmission. Clearly, this was timed precisely to fit with the UK government's plan to open schools in September despite criticism from parents and teachers and, as argued earlier, was counterintuitive. The sad fact was that the WHO's prediction that Europe would see a rise in COVID-19 cases over October and November became true and cases continued to climb.

By this point in the year, the world had suffered an economic shock. The exact cost of the pandemic was unknown, and after all, it was not over yet. Companies and workers in many countries had been protected by state aid. The World Economic Forum had postponed the 2021 Davos summit from January to summer. Travel and tourism had been big losers. The UN Secretary-General Antonio Guterres, announced that $320 billion had been lost in exports in the global tourism industry due to the disruption caused by the pandemic. US giant American Airlines announced it would cut 19,000 jobs in the US in October unless the US government extended its stimulus package for the airline industry. In the UK, the spending watchdog declared that the UK COVID-19 bill had cost the UK Government a whopping £210 billion. Fears over a second UK lockdown in the autumn wiped £50 billion off the FTSE 100 Index.

The family were brilliant at looking after me. Amanda did what she could over the weekends and worried about returning to work after my first weekend at home. She had become a head teacher while I was in intensive care and had spent too many days and nights worrying about me and looking after me. It was time for her to return to what she now needed to do, to be a head teacher and get the children back to learning in school after the lockdown and summer holiday. Amanda rose to the head teacher challenge and worked hard to get to know her new team in a new school. Now she was the boss of the school and everyone looked to her for the answers. As ever, Amanda took this in her stride, whilst at the same time reducing the amount of direct care she provided for me as well as helping me become increasingly independent.

Anna and Lawrence, and Colin took me places in their cars, sometimes for practical things such as banking but also for more enjoyable reasons such as for coffee or a drink at one of our local pubs. Callum and Douglas came over fairly regularly. Callum would potter around and help out with some of my former duties around the house. When I was still in hospital, Amanda had organised a group of family and friends to do quite a bit of work in the garden over the summer to tidy it up. She restructured our terrace area so I would be able to enjoy it on my return home and sit there with friends or family to enjoy a coffee outside in fine weather.

The 'Eat Out to Help Out' scheme in the August had helped kick-start the hospitality industry that had suffered terribly under the spring lockdown. I made use of this with many friends, and Amanda and I also ate out on many occasions. We finally held Colin's 21st birthday at a local restaurant and although I have no memory of his birthday, it was a time of celebration for many reasons. Although I struggled to sit on hard restaurant chairs due to the limited amount of padding in my rear, I had the cushion from the wheelchair that went everywhere with me. We held a garden party for those closest to us a few weeks after leaving hospital and it was lovely to celebrate being home with family and friends. The only person who could not join the party was my mother who was too frail to travel the 80 miles to join the fun.

The UK government pinned its hopes on 'Operation Moonshot', a £100 billion mass-testing programme to avoid a second lockdown. It received an unprecedented level of criticism as the funding equated to 75% of the annual NHS budget in England with contracts being awarded without parliamentary scrutiny to friends and associates of those in central government, and in the end, it failed and had to be subsumed into the NHS Test and Trace system, which was itself failing to meet the promised expectations. Politicians continued to flaunt the rules around travel and caught the public eye. Dominic Cummings remained in the spotlight and was joined by Margaret Ferrier, an SNP MP who was suspended after she took a train from London to Scotland despite testing positive for COVID-19. Such breaches were not confined to Britain, the Irish Minister for Agriculture Dara Calleary resigned after breaking COVID-19 guidelines with his attendance at a golf society dinner. Despite having denied COVID-19, Donald Trump and the US First Lady tested positive on 2 October. How sick he was remains conjectural as he was showcased as an in-patient and on discharge to the world's media. Trump couldn't have been very ill as he held a large outdoor rally in Florida only a matter of days following discharge. Demonstrating that COVID-19 was not confined to humans, Denmark and other mink-rearing countries were asked to cull a million mink after coronavirus infections were found among animals in mink farms. Later, COVID-19 would be found to have been transmitted from humans to cats.

My sleeping slowly improved and I started to be able to roll over in bed and change position whilst asleep, rather than having to wake myself up to do so and then struggling to sleep through the rest of the night. Unfortunately, another significant problem arose as the nerve function in my ankles and feet started to return. I was troubled by horrific levels of neuropathy where my ankles and feet felt as if they were being attacked with blowtorches pumping out extreme cold, rather than heat. I sat up on many nights wanting to cut my feet off at my ankles with a power saw. Realising that this was not a normal thought process, I eventually asked my GP to medicate me for this. I had been his only patient who had suffered critical care COVID-19 infection. He had phoned me a few days after discharge to let me know that he knew about my plight from the TV and newspaper articles and would provide what I needed, all I had to do was call the surgery. He put me on an increasingly strong dose of Gabapentin to block out the nerve signals from my ankles and feet, which worked, although I did not like the side effects.

After two months at home, I no longer needed the bathroom equipment and kitchen perch stool, nebuliser and the wheelchair. It took some organisation to have these picked up and returned but I did not want to keep them unnecessarily as other patients would also need them. I did, however, need to hold on to the walking stick, now dubbed Sticky McStick in a parody of Boaty McBoatface, the underwater polar exploration boat that was named in a somewhat controversial online poll in 2016. Sticky became a constant companion on all journeys from the house and Sherlock had a reluctant sense of respect for it as the tap on the ground became the beat for walking.

I was eager to drive again. Amanda was less than enthusiastic and by now had transformed from being the protagonist who had been protecting me to the carer constraining me. I understood this so discussed driving with the rehabilitation team around me. Nobody wanted to take the ultimate decision of deciding if I was safe to drive but interestingly, none of the conditions I had endured were of relevance to the UK Driver and Vehicle Licensing Agency and, therefore, I did not have to alert them or my insurance company. I discussed driving with Dr McDonald, who had become my respiratory consultant now looking after all follow up for me via a video appointment, and he saw no reason why I should not soon be driving. On finishing the call, I went straight out and took the car for a drive, without difficulty. It felt a bit like my driving test, but I got the hang of the controls fairly quickly. I was relieved that I could still drive after such a long time and this provided me with renewed freedom. I no longer had to rely on lifts from everyone and this represented a big step in my quest to be independent again.

I could now drive to the physiotherapy gym for appointments with Kathryn and the activity level stepped up again. I was now doing cardio circuits in the gym with various stretches and, following a second respiratory appointment with Dr McDonald, Kathryn and Amanda were to restart chest physiotherapy to help clear my lungs of phlegm and spit. Rather surprisingly, this was now much less unpleasant than before and I attributed this to much stronger muscles in my ribs and diaphragm, which must have become equally as weak as all the other muscles in my body. The twice-weekly gym sessions always overran. During the session we had conversations that varied from religion to the US elections, covering sport, current affairs and, of course, the Scottish weather in between. When Kathryn was on holiday, one of the team stepped in. They were equally conversational and likewise expected me to work hard in the gym but more importantly to work hard on my own, in between gym sessions. I drove myself to occupational therapy appointments and had a consultation with rheumatology due to persistent stiffness, pain and limitation of movement in many of my joints, particularly my hands and feet. Woefully, I was diagnosed with osteoporosis as well as arthritis and these limited the amount of recovery significantly. I wanted to walk more and be more active with my hands, but my feet and hands limited what I could do. I am hopeful that there will be a cure or, at least, some relief down the line.

More positively, I saw Dr McDonald for a respiratory follow up three months after discharge and having examined a new CT scan of my lungs along with breathing tests, he was delighted with my progress to date. The sickest survivor had also made the greatest recovery of the cohort of patients in my health board thus far and he was keen to see how far my recovery could stretch. Dr McDonald encouraged me to refocus my goals from 50% improvement or so to as much recovery as possible and therefore the rehabilitation journey has no end date as yet. There had been much discussion on the collection of debilitating symptoms that even people with relatively mild COVID-19 disease experienced - Long COVID-19 - and although I decided that I would not suffer from it, Dr McDonald counselled that I had to admit to suffering from some of its symptoms.

Media interest continued for months after returning home with many of the newspapers that had carried the story at various stages running follow-up stories about my rehabilitation journey. Similarly, the dental and orthodontic journals were interested in the story and I, therefore, had the opportunity to demonstrate the effect of the rehabilitation journey as well as the hospital journey to my colleagues, many who were close friends and had been willing me on throughout ill health and recovery. Some of the newspapers and the BBC news website also ran further follow-up stories at Christmas and beyond giving me an opportunity to recall how much progress there had been to date and consider how much more I would want to strive for. One of the Scottish Sunday newspapers ran a story called 'The Great Survivor', with contributions from those who had provided so much medical and rehabilitation care for me, which was touching.

I had been winning the rehabilitation battle but knew the physiotherapy with Kathryn and operational therapy work with Laura would continue at home for many, many months ahead. I was vaccinated against COVID-19 as there was no way I could go through the experience again. I recognised that COVID-19 had been a challenging period in our lives as it had been for so many people, but I became determined that it would not define my identity. As I recovered, I returned to work as a consultant orthodontist and went to the golf driving range before Christmas 2020. Despite lockdown over winter 2021, I went skiing locally and started cycling with the aid of an e-bike and covered hundreds of miles. Motorcycling remained elusive as Amanda was, not surprisingly, resistant to me risking my life. I climbed a local 3000-foot mountain on the anniversary of falling ill with Lawrence, Colin, Piers and, of course, Sherlock. It felt incredible to stand at the top and look south to Ninewells Hospital in Dundee and North East to Aberdeen from the summit. I felt that I had conquered COVID-19, even though my lungs were still damaged and had limited my progress up the mountain. I had re-entered a different world to the one I left abruptly in March and on returning to work, my office was exactly as I had left it with the laptop still plugged in and papers lying on the desk. My good friends at work spoiled me on my first day back with some lovely presents waiting on my desk for me. What a treat. I felt guilty that various aspects of my work had ended up having to be picked up by my colleagues.

Our family was, in 2021, joined by Sherlock Bones' direct brother, Watson, another yellow Labrador, and together they took us on a variety of adventures and my rehabilitation journey accelerated.

I was pleased to note the WHO's Director General, Tedros Adhanom Ghebreyesus, announced that an international team of experts would visit Wuhan to study the origins of COVID-19. At the time of writing, their report is awaited. Viruses, like all lifeforms with genetic material, constantly mutate. Fortunately, the vast majority of virus mutations die out and of the 12,000 variants that had been detected since the initial outbreak of COVID-19 in Wuhan, only five had proved of significance. One variant from Spanish farm workers (20A.EU1) spread rapidly throughout Europe in autumn 2020 and another, found in Kent in the South East of England (20I/501Y.V1), became prevalent - it had 70% greater transmissibility than the initial virus type. The South African variant (20H/501Y.V2) was similar though subtly distinct to the Kent variant. The Brazil variant (B.1.1.28) emerged in Latin America during 2020 and with four mutations noted to date, this variant caused concern across Europe. The eponymous Indian variant (B.1.617) infected over 18 million people and was devastating to communities throughout the sub-continent. The hope was that all sub-types that had been identified, and those yet to be identified, would continue to responsive to the vaccines. Reassuringly, the vaccine manufacturers announced they could modify their products relatively quickly to address the variants as they emerge.

COVID-19 has been very much the disease of the moment, emanating from a crowded city in a newly prosperous and well-connected China before spreading to the rest of the world within a matter of months. We should not forget that our response to COVID-19 has been both hyper-modern and at the same time medieval. Nevertheless, we have missed the opportunity to use certain historical methods of virus control. The word quarantine comes from the Italian phrase *quaranta giorni* meaning 40 days, a period of special significance in the Bible, that of purification during the period of temptation in the desert now marked by Lent. This was certainly significant to the medieval city state of Venice, a Catholic city; merchant ships were required to moor offshore for 40 days to avoid disease being brought into the overcrowded city. Perhaps something to learn in today's society even though not everyone would want to spend a full 40 days in quarantine now. Scientists around the world have been in constant communication throughout the pandemic and have used cutting-edge laboratory tools to rapidly sequence the genome of each new variant. They have shared information about virulence and collaborated on possible counter-measures and vaccines, much more quickly than could ever have been done before.

Despite the early warning, when the virus arrived, the western world looked on, rather than asking China the key questions and planning effective measures for prevention of transmission. In the end, the only effective response the west could muster was to shut down society and turn off the assembly line and supply chain of global capitalism and consumerism. Apart from text messaging for information, videoconferencing tools, home shopping and home subscription TV services, what we have used so far is not that different from what our ancestors might have used to halt an outbreak of either the Justinianic or Black Plagues. The result of our actions was the same as an anti-cancer drug in slowing the growth of a tumour, by reducing the expansion of the global economy and limiting freedom of movement.

SARS and MERS gave us a taste of what could come but we missed the opportunity to predict another bigger pandemic, which rapidly became panic. The world needs to strengthen the antennae of global health, to ensure that any emerging virus in the future, which is guaranteed, will be stopped more quickly. My own view is that COVID-19 will not go away since it is so infectious and, after all, the only virus that we have eradicated as a human race is smallpox. The world will have to live with COVID-19 in the same way as it does with influenza, with vaccinating the vulnerable as well as using precautions to prevent transmission. The prospect of a third wave and beyond in the UK is frightening. It seems surprising that the budget of the WHO, the agency with the responsibility for safeguarding the health of the world's 7.8 billion citizens, is only the same as a large US urban hospital. Locally, public health systems need additional capacity in terms of human and physical resources to be able to deal with surge capacity. Nightingale hospitals were heralded as the potential solution in the UK, but were not used to capacity in the first wave and many had been either scaled back or removed, just as the second more intensive wave struck, with many later becoming temporary mass vaccination centres. And, of course, we need to ensure the lessons of COVID-19 are learnt, for all too often the initial shock has a huge impact on people, political promises are made but are then forgotten as the memory of the outbreak fades over time. It is important that our political leaders ensure we all learn the lessons from COVID-19 so we do not repeat the mistakes with the same human cost.

To date, there have been over 167 million cases of COVID-19 and over 3 million deaths worldwide, fortunately far fewer than the half billion people who have died over the last 2,000 years from other viruses. It is worth recognising that the majority of people have recovered and somehow I was one of them. Interestingly, though, the infection and death rate among countries has not followed the traditional models for infection as yet where poorer countries have greater levels of disease and death. Rather, many less-developed countries have fared better due to sensible precautions being adopted to prevent widespread infection along with compliant societies following the rules closely. Unfortunately, the UK does not look good in world terms with nearly 5 million cases and approaching 130,000 deaths. The proportion of the UK population who have been infected is now the worst of all the developed countries in the world. Sad reading, but true.

Vaccines became the way out of the pandemic since the human herd seemed incapable of following the rules and regulations preventing transmission. Unlike other vaccines, the COVID-19 vaccines were not based on a weakened or denatured form of the virus but have used the so-called 'spike' proteins on the surface of the virus particle to produce antibodies and other immune reactions. The protein is either injected directly, via the denatured chimpanzee cold virus (AstraZeneca) with the COVID-19 DNA being used to produce the spike protein, or using genetic material called mRNA to trigger human cells to produce the spike protein such as the Pfizer-BioNTech and Moderna vaccines. Vaccines started being administered in the UK, Bahrain, Canada, the USA and many other countries in December 2020. With nearly 200 in development at 95% effectiveness, the COVAX programme will be the most ambitious vaccination programme to date. Vaccinating all 7.8 billion people on the planet will take time so eradicating COVID-19 will not be instantaneous. I was fortunate to receive both doses of the vaccine relatively early in the programme since I work for the NHS, with my elderly mother also being vaccinated at a relatively early stage as well. There were concerns about the very small risk of blood clots being caused by the AstraZeneca vaccine and despite limited data, many countries chose to restrict the use to specific age groups or use an alternative. I wondered if there was some politics involved around Brexit but the vaccine strategy got the UK back on track and restrictions were eased as spring 2021 unfolded in the UK, much to everyone's relief at being released from the third lockdown. India, as one of the world's largest manufacturers of vaccines was sadly crippled by the raging bull of the Indian variant whilst the majority of vaccine supplies were exported to richer countries.

I discovered when writing this book that the average hospital stay of a COVID patient was eight days, the average ventilator time was 16 days and the average post-ICU journey was four weeks. My journey was massive and I appreciate that I am lucky to be alive now. Whilst the journey was by no means one that I would like anyone to repeat, I recognise, as I reflect down the line, that it was a privilege to have made it. I hope that the politicians around the UK who have been culpable in the death of so many citizens recognise that there was a considerably larger amount of work they could have done to reduce the death toll. My hope is that they move the agenda from infection to injection and then to prevention rather than playing party politics and creating ever-changing geographically confusing rules and restrictions which are hard for the population to follow.

My NHS heroes had not only saved my life but have helped me rebuild it. They took me from the worst point in my life where I had, in the words of the song, been 'knocking on heaven's door,' through the maze of critical illness and rehabilitation to a point where life was for living. I realise I have so much to be grateful for and my heart continues to go out to families who have not had a similar fortunate outcome. I am now in the second half of my life having turned 50 and, as with all good games, expect that the second half will be more fulfilling than the first. The home run was just that. As a family, we had completed quite a journey to get me home in the space of a year and although I am not quite back to where I started, I have had the journey of my life - one which has shaped the future for Amanda and me in such a positive way.

I had been dying to live, quite literally.

END

About the Authors

Grant McIntyre is a Professor and Consultant in orthodontics at the University of Dundee Dental Hospital & School and his wife Amanda is a head teacher of a primary school in Perth, Scotland. Grant and Amanda were aware of the new virus that had emerged from Wuhan in China at the end of 2019 and as this moved progressively west through countries such as Iran and Italy, Grant and Amanda spent considerable time preparing for the emerging pandemic in their professional lives. It was a tragic irony that Grant fell ill with COVID-19 during the last week of March 2020 and was put into a medical coma. Although everyone fought for Grant to survive, COVID-19 and his ensuing body's cytokine storm immune response nearly killed him outright. He suffered a number of medical complications including kidney failure, a collapsed lung and sepsis while in intensive care which were all potentially fatal. Somehow everyone's prayers were answered when there were finally signs of life after 50 days on ECMO life support. He was and remains the sickest survivor of COVID-19 in Scotland and with the amazing medical, nursing and rehabilitation teams, he finally left hospital after four months. Grant made a miraculous recovery and managed to rebuild his life with the support of Amanda, his remarkable family and tremendous friends. Grant and Amanda tell their horrific COVID-19 journey and their experience of COVID-19 in this book along with their perspectives on surviving critical illness and the global response to the pandemic. If you don't believe in COVID-19, masks or vaccines, you should read this book. It will open your eyes to the personal story of a family who were fortunate in the conquest of a vicious infective disease.

TIPPERMUIR BOOKS

Tippermuir Books Ltd (est. 2009) is an independent publishing company based in Perth, Scotland.

PUBLISHING HISTORY

Spanish Thermopylae (2009)

Battleground Perthshire (2009)

Perth: Street by Street (2012)

Born in Perthshire (2012)

In Spain with Orwell (2013)

Trust (2014)

Perth: As Others Saw Us (2014)

Love All (2015)

A Chocolate Soldier (2016)

The Early Photographers of Perthshire (2016)

Taking Detective Novels Seriously: The Collected
Crime Reviews of Dorothy L Sayers (2017)

Walking with Ghosts (2017)

No Fair City: Dark Tales from Perth's Past (2017)

The Tale o the Wee Mowdie that wantit tae ken
wha keeched on his heid (2017)

Hunters: Wee Stories from the Crescent:
A Reminiscence of Perth's Hunter Crescent (2017)

A Little Book of Carol's (2018)

Flipstones (2018)

Perth: Scott's Fair City:
The Fair Maid of Perth & Sir Walter Scott –
A Celebration & Guided Tour (2018)

God, Hitler, and Lord Peter Wimsey: Selected Essays,
Speeches and Articles by Dorothy L Sayers (2019)

Perth & Kinross: A Pocket Miscellany:
A Companion for Visitors and Residents (2019)

The Piper of Tobruk:
Pipe Major Robert Roy, MBE, DCM (2019)

The 'Gig Docter o Athole':
Dr William Irvine & The Irvine Memorial Hospital (2019)

Afore the Highlands: The Jacobites in Perth, 1715–16 (2019)

'Where Sky and Summit Meet':
Flight Over Perthshire – A History: Tales of Pilots,
Airfields, Aeronautical Feats, & War (2019)

Diverted Traffic (2020)

Authentic Democracy:
An Ethical Justification of Anarchism (2020)

'If Rivers Could Sing': A Scottish River Wildlife Journey.
A Year in the Life of the River Devon as it flows
through the Counties of Perthshire,
Kinross-shire & Clackmannanshire (2020)

A Squatter o Bairnrhymes (2020)

In a Sma Room Songbook:
From the Poems by William Soutar
(2020)

The Nicht Afore Christmas:
The much-loved yuletide tale in Scots (2020)

Ice Cold Blood (eBook, 2021)

FORTHCOMING

The Perth Riverside Nursery & Beyond:
A Spirit of Enterprise and Improvement
(Elspeth Bruce and Pat Kerr, 2021)

Fatal Duty – The Scottish Police Force to 1952:
Cop killers, Killer Cops & More
(Gary Knight, 2021)

William Soutar: Collected Poetry, Volume I
(Published Work)
(Kirsteen McCue and Paul S Philippou (editors), 2021)

William Soutar: Collected Poetry, Volume II
(Unpublished Work)
(Kirsteen McCue and Paul S Philippou (editors), 2022)

Beyond the Swelkie:
A Collection of New Poems and Writings to Mark the
Centenary of George Mackay Brown (1921–1996)
(Jim Mackintosh & Paul S Philippou (editors), 2021)

A Scottish Wildlife Odyssey (Keith Broomfield, 2021)

The Shanter Legacy:
The Search for the Grey Mare's Tail
(Garry Stewart, 2021)

All Tippermuir Books titles are
available from bookshops and online booksellers.
They can also be purchased directly
with free postage & packing [UK only] –
(minimum charges for overseas delivery) from
www.tippermuirbooks.co.uk

Tippermuir Books Ltd can be contacted at
mail@tippermuirbooks.co.uk

Lullaby
Press